086458

W9-ADF-753

7115 SAG, CMRB 2407
APO New York 09057

THE LIBRARY
ST. MARY'S COLLEGE OF MARYLAND
ST. MARY'S CITY, MARYLAND 20686

SUEZ: TEN YEARS AFTER

SUEZ

Pantheon Books • A DIVISION OF RANDOM HOUSE • NEW YO

EN YEARS AFTER

troduced by Peter Calvocoressi

lited by·Anthony Moncrieff

FIRST AMERICAN EDITION

© Copyright, 1966, 1967, by the British Broadcasting Corporation and Paul Bareau, Thomas Barman, Michel Bar-Zohar, General Andre Beaufre, David Ben-Gurion, Robert Bowie, Peter Calvocoressi, General Moshe Dayan, Hans-Eberhard Dingels, Henry Durant, Abba Eban, John Erickson, Andre Fontaine, Elie Kedourie, Jon Kimche, Tom Little, President Nasser, H. G. Nicholas, Anthony Nutting, Christian Pineau, W. R. Polk, Robert Rhodes James, Lord Robens, Terence Robertson, Robert Stephens, P. Varikiotis, and C. M. Woodhouse. All rights reserved under International and Pan-American Copyright Conventions. Published in New York by Pantheon Books, a division of Random House, Inc., and in London, England, by the British Broadcasting Corporation.

Library of Congress Catalog Card Number: 67-23530

Manufactured in the United States of America
By The Colonial Press, Inc., Clinton, Mass.

BY ARRANGEMENT WITH THE BRITISH BROADCASTING CORPORATION

12-11-78

FEB 11 1979

Contents

Contributors

The following took part in one or more of the eight programmes:

Paul Bareau, No. 1; T. G. Barman, No. 1; Michel Bar-Zohar, Nos. 3 & 4; General Beaufre, No. 1; David Ben-Gurion, No. 3; Professor Robert Bowie, Nos. 1 & 2; General Dayan, No. 4; Hans-Eberhard Dingels, No. 8; Henry Durant, No. 1; Abba Eban, No. 3; John Erickson, Nos. 1, 2 & 6; Andre Fontaine, Nos. 2, 3 & 4; Elie Kedourie, Nos. 3 & 4; Jon Kimche, Nos. 3 & 4; Tom Little, No. 2; President Nasser, Nos. 1 & 2; H. G. Nicholas, No. 7; Anthony Nutting, No. 8; Christian Pineau, Nos. 2, 3 & 4; Professor W. R. Polk, No. 8; Robert Rhodes James, No. 5; Lord Robens, No. 4; Terence Robertson, Nos. 3 & 4; Robert Stephens, No. 2; Professor P. Vatikiotis, No. 2; The Hon. C. M. Woodhouse, No. 1.

Recordings from BBC Sound Archives of Imre Nagy and Radio Rakoczi, President D. Eisenhower, Selwyn Lloyd and Hugh Gaitskell are included in the first programme, and of Sir Anthony Eden in the first and second programmes. Extracts have also been taken from a despatch of Sir Charles Keightley (No. 1), a letter by President Eisenhower (No. 1), General Dayan's Diaries (Nos. 3 & 4), *Full Circle* (No. 4), and Hansard (No. 4).

This book is based on the series of BBC programmes originated and produced by Anthony Moncrieff.

Foreword

This book contains the texts of eight programmes which I prepared for the BBC's Third Programme in 1966. They are reprinted here as they were delivered, subject only to verbal alterations by contributors who were given the opportunity to rephrase for publication what they had said in interviews. I should like, however, in presenting them to an American public and by way of preface, to say something about their origin and purpose and to venture one or two further reflections.

The immediate occasion for the series was the tenth anniversary of the nationalization of the Suez Canal Company by President Nasser and the war which ensued three months later. But it was not my intention, or the intention of my producer, Anthony Moncrieff, simply to revive past controversies. What we wished to do was to experiment with broadcasting as a technique for the study of what, paradoxically to some people, is called contemporary history. Much is known about the antecedents, the course and the consequences of the Suez war. Other things remain obscure. There is nothing odd about that, nor is it a peculiarity of contemporary history, for the same could be said about the battle of Hastings, whose ninth centenary was being celebrated in the same year. What is different about contemporary history is the fact that many of the actors remain as much alive as the student himself. They can be interrogated; their answers can be put alongside their actions, and also alongside statements which they themselves have made earlier. On broadcasting, as nowhere else, they are heard saying things in their own voices. They can neither deny their own words nor complain of misrepresentation. And broadcasting has a second unique characteristic; it can reproduce and recall the sounds of the times, and therefore their immediacy, in a way which even photography, let alone the printed word, cannot emulate. In this series, for example, we reproduced the agonized call for help which came, in English, from Hungary as the Russian tanks were moving on Budapest. We established that the two crises of those days—Suez and Hungary—were in fact independent, but our Suez chronicle would have been incomplete if we had not found a way of recalling the impact of the Hungarian rising and the sense of bewilderment and guilt felt by many in the West who supposed that, but for Suez, something might have been done for Hungary. Emotions are potent but evanescent. Nothing in the past is more difficult to recapture, and for this reason the actions of leaders or of crowds often appear bizarre to a later generation which cannot imagine the atmosphere which animated them. Sounds help.

The material for these broadcasts, then, was provided by many months of research in the usual documentary sources with which the contemporary historian is familiar, and, secondly, by interviews with statesmen, service chiefs, officials, journalists and others whose professional activities in various countries were a part of the story or whose subsequent reflections might illuminate it. The amount of material collected in this way was considerable. As students of this type of inquiry will know, some of it could not be used directly or be attributed. I should guess that what we eventually used, and what now appears in this book, amounts to no more than a tenth of the whole. There has therefore been editorial discrimination, just as there was an initial discrimination in the choice of whom to approach. But it does not follow that those who do not figure in the programmes were not asked to do so. Lord Avon (Anthony Eden) and Mr. Selwyn Lloyd, for example, were invited to contribute but preferred not to; President Eisenhower, who was in hospital when the programmes were being prepared, also declined after pondering the matter for some weeks, but we were able to use the second volume of his memoirs which appeared at this time. The resulting picture is not the last word on Suez (after all the last word has not yet been said on the battle of Hastings), but its accuracy and fairness have not been called in question publicly or privately, so far as I know, notwithstanding that the programmes were originally listened to by record audiences, were subsequently repeated both *in toto* in the Third Programme and in an abbreviated version in the BBC's Home Service, and were printed in digested form in *The Listener*.

The debate on the Suez War has consisted of a central core plus tangential issues which have varied from country to country. Americans who read these broadcasts, designed for a British audience, may feel that the tangential issues of special interest in the United States have received only scant attention or none. I wish therefore to add a few words on topics which are not discussed in the broadcasts. I have in mind these questions: Did the United States let down its allies? Has Washington in effect adopted a double standard, requiring advance consultation by allies (Suez), but without reciprocity (Cuba, Vietnam)? And not only advance consultation but the abnegation of certain methods, i.e. the use of force, which it continues to permit to itself? Was the American stance over Suez dictated by oilmen? Did Washington tacitly swap Suez for Hungary, condemning the former and condoning the latter because it feared a general war? In sum, were the actions of the Administration governed less than at first sight appeared by principle and more by particular pressures or pragmatic manoeuvre (*combinazione* or adjustment, to borrow an expressive term from Italian politics)?

It is necessary to draw a distinction between circumstances and motives. Any industrial country will pay attention, in the conduct of policy, to the fact that it is industrialized and has industrial interests. It does not follow that its industrialists can sway its politicians. A country with direct investments in oil will respond the more readily to special arguments about the need not to endanger oil installations, but again it does not follow that these considerations or the men who advance them dominate policy-makers, and it can be argued that the main difference between a country with oil investments and a country without them is not that the first will be intent on protecting these investments and the latter careless of their fate, but that the first will feel an obligation itself to safeguard the flow of oil while the latter (assuming that it too uses oil) will be anxious to see the former doing the job. The question that intrigues is not whether these considerations are proper but whether they are allowed too much weight and lead a government to do things which it would otherwise not do and—a separate question—which it ought not to do. The question has arisen in a variety of contexts involving not only oilmen but bankers, armament manufacturers, farmers and others. It is in the nature of things very difficult to answer in any given case and I can only say that I did not find evidence that American policy in the Suez crisis was what it was because of American oil interests. In general it seems to me that, in the United States and other advanced industrial countries, the public servants constitute an autonomous profession and that politicians of the top rank are much more influenced by the bureaucracy than the plutocracy. This is not to say that the Administration was not very conscious of the threat to the flow of oil from Arab sources if Britain and France attacked Egypt. This threat was obvious and it was an ingredient in the American decision to come out against the allies and, in the case of Britain, to put the financial screws on; but it is neither necessary to postulate, nor possible to find convincing evidence for, a sinister plot by American oilmen to use the crisis to oust British and French competitors. What they hoped for is another matter.

The argument, which has also been advanced, that the U.S. Administration resolved to stop Britain and France in mid-course because of the Hungarian crisis is also difficult to sustain. This argument supposes that, had there been no Hungarian crisis, Washington would have allowed Britain and France to carry on, but that Hungary created something like a panic in which the Administration, fearing an extension of the fighting in Europe, decided that the fighting in the Middle East must be snuffed out. The gravamen of this charge is hypocrisy. The Administration cannot be blamed for trying to stop wars but it could be blamed for pretending to intervene in the Suez war for one reason when its real reasons were different: juggled motives. Moreover, subsequent actions in Cuba and Vietnam have suggested that, to put it mildly, the American distaste for the use of force is not as potent in some instances as others and even that force is a political weapon which, in the American view, may properly be used by the United States but not by others: a double standard.

These complaints add up to the charge of being a bad ally. Americans have been known to complain in their turn that their allies have not been as loyal as they should have been—notably when it came to fighting in Korea or in Vietnam. What are the obligations of an ally? Is it enough for an ally to do what it has contracted to do in the treaty of alliance? Or does alliance import also the obligations of friendship, so that an ally may be expected to give aid and comfort in unconvenanted and unforeseen situations? There is no clear answer to these questions because, for all that they look like general moral propositions, they are essentially political questions in disguise and every ally will weigh its course of action in each particular instance by a number of criteria (including moral ones). It seems to me impossible to argue that Washington let down its allies in 1956 except upon the basis that the United States was bound, as an ally, to support Britain and France in whatever they were doing, however silly: 'my ally right or wrong'. On the evidence available the United States opposed the use of force on practical politico-moral grounds (they were set out in the broadcast series by Professor Robert R. Bowie) and not because of the Hungarian crisis. There was no obligation that I can see of any kind upon the Administration to do otherwise, the more so since its allies deliberately kept it in the dark. This, *qua* allies, they were entitled to do, just as the United States properly acted on its own, albeit in very different circumstances, in the Cuban missile crisis. Britain and France were entitled to proceed—in the sense that they were not contractually precluded from proceeding—without American approbation, although they were exceedingly foolish to do so. But if this view of the matter is correct, then Americans have to be careful neither to expect a higher degree of loyalty than they have themselves extended nor to feel aggrieved when they do not get it.

Friends and allies must also, I suggest, be careful not to object to particular actions in general terms. Some American (and other) condemnations of the use of force against Egypt in 1956 were couched in language which condemned force in all circumstances. But a blanket condemnation of a particular method, unrelated to circumstances or to objectives, is more often than not extremely implausible. Absolute non-violence may be a tenable position (this is not the place to argue it), but it was certainly not the basis of most of the critics of Britain and France in 1956, whatever some of them seemed to be saying. Indignation, however, produced overstatement, and the overstatements of American origin boomeranged in later crises where, as at Suez, one of the friends—who was also, although in another context, an ally—disliked what the other was doing. The use of force, whether at Suez or in Cuba, the Dominican Republic or Vietnam, is judged by most observers pragmatically: surrounding circumstances are more telling than general propositions. But the general propositions advanced in one crisis become part of the surrounding circumstances of the next, bedevilling judgement—and alliances.

I do not mean to say that an alliance needs no cement apart from the writing in the treaty, nor that an alliance covering certain fields of activity leaves the relations between the allies in other fields wholly untouched. There is no clear line between the obligations of alliance and those of friendship. Alliance and friendship are not coterminous and each may even exist without the other, but for the most part an alliance, however limited its specific obligations, needs continuing good will. This good will, however, must be won and maintained by sensible performance in times of crisis and not by undiscriminating loyalty at such times. Measured thus, Anglo-American good will was jeopardized in 1956 not by the American government but by the British. Measured thus, it was not jeopardized by the American government in the Cuban missiles crisis but was put to some strain, temporary and slight, over the Dominican Republic, and to much severer and more enduring strain over Vietnam. The rule which I would like to see affirmed by these crises is that the primary obligation is on the leading actor to act sensibly and not on the ally to react with a preordained loyalty.

One final remark: it seemed strange to many Europeans that Americans should be so much more preoccupied with their elections than with two separate threatening wars, especially as the re-election of President Eisenhower was a foregone conclusion.

PETER CALVOCORESSI

A Chronology

26 July	President Nasser announced that the Suez Canal Company had been nationalized, and that the funds obtained from operating the canal would be used to finance the Aswan High Dam.
30 July	The British Prime Minister, Sir Anthony Eden, stated that Single-Power control of the Canal was totally unacceptable.
1 August	The American Secretary of State, Mr Dulles, arrived in London to join Three-Power talks on crisis with representatives of Britain and France. (Talks ended on 3 August with agreement to call an International Conference in London.)
2 August	British Government announced state of emergency and recall of some reservists. In House of Commons, Labour Party warned Government that it would not support use of force except in accordance with the Charter of the United Nations.
16 August	International Conference in London. Mr Dulles put forward the Western plan for an International Board to run the Canal.
20 August	India proposed alternative plan, entailing the setting up of a consultative committee of Canal users leaving the Canal under Eygptian control.
23 August	The Dulles Plan, with minor amendments, adopted by eighteen of the Nations attending the London Conference. A Committee of five Nations, under Mr Menzies (Australian Prime Minister), appointed to 'present and explain' the plan to President Nasser.
29 August	Announced that French troops were to be stationed in Cyprus.
3 September	Mr Menzies and President Nasser held first meeting in Cairo. Proposals finally rejected on 9 September.
10 September	M. Guy Mollet and M. Christian Pineau (French Prime Minister and Foreign Minister) visit London for talks.
11 September	The Suez Canal Company issued a statement authorizing its European pilots to withdraw. President Eisenhower told a press conference that the United States would not become involved in a Middle East War.

12 September In London, Parliament – specially recalled – discussed the Suez crisis; and on 13 September rejected the Opposition motion of censure. Sir Anthony Eden, in conjunction with the Americans and French, announced plans for setting up a Suez Canal Users' Association (SCUA).

15 September The European pilots left Egypt.

19 September Second International Conference opened in London of eighteen Nations supporting the Dulles Plan to consider the scheme for a Canal Users' Association. Agreement reached on 21 September.

23 September Britain and France referred the Suez dispute to the Security Council of the United Nations.

24 September Egypt lodged complaint with Security Council against Anglo-French concentrations of troops and threats of war.

26 September Security Council met, and decided to consider both the Anglo-French and Egyptian complaints. Sir Anthony Eden and Mr Selwyn Lloyd (British Foreign Secretary) visit Paris for talks.

1 October First meeting of SCUA in London.

5 October In New York, Security Council began consideration of Suez question. Sir Anthony Eden goes to hospital.

10 October Security Council went into secret session. Six principles for management of Canal agreed in private meetings between Foreign Ministers of Britain, France and Egypt.

13 October Security Council and Egypt accepted the Six principles as basis of agreement. Egypt, however, refused to accept British resolution that Eighteen Nation Plan corresponded to requirements of these principles.

16 October Sir Anthony Eden and Mr Selwyn Lloyd visited Paris for talks on Middle East with M. Guy Mollet and M. Christian Pineau.

21 October General election in Jordan.

23 October M. Pineau visited London for talks. (During this same week, it is alleged, French and Israeli leaders met secretly near Paris and were joined by British representatives.)

28 October   Israel ordered general mobilization of reserves.

29 October   Israeli forces crossed Egyptian border and attacked positions in Sinai desert.

30 October   Anglo-French ultimatum to Israel and Egypt:
       to cease hostilities by land, sea and air;
       to withdraw troops ten miles from Suez Canal; and to allow occupation by Anglo-French forces of Port Said, Ismailia and Suez (in accordance with Articles 4 and 6 of the Suez Pact of 1954 drawn up when Suez Base was returned to Egypt).
       Ultimatum accepted conditionally by Israel and rejected by Egypt.
       Britain and France vetoed (1) U.S. resolution in Security Council calling for a cease-fire, withdrawal of Israeli forces, and calling on all United Nations members to refrain from using force in the area, and (2) Soviet resolution calling for cease-fire and withdrawal of Israeli forces.

US wanted

31 October   Anglo-French air forces attacked Egyptian airfields. Security Council called emergency meeting of General Assembly.

1 November   Israeli forces almost sealed off Gaza strip: claimed Egyptians in rout in Sinai.

2 November   British and French claimed the Egyptian Air Force had been practically destroyed. Israeli forces mopping up in Sinai. United Nations General Assembly called for cease-fire, and withdrawal of attacking forces. M. Pineau visits London for talks.

3 November   Britain and France replied to General Assembly giving conditions for a cease-fire. Israel accepted cease-fire, provided Egypt did the same.

4 November   It was announced that the Egyptians had blocked the Suez Canal.
       United Nations Secretary General drew attention of Britain, France, Egypt and Israel to resolutions before Assembly calling for cease-fire and asking for halt to all military operations by 0500 G.M.T.
       M. Pineau visits London for talks. Egypt replied accepting cease-fire; Israel's reply asked a series of questions about Egypt's intentions. (The same day

	Soviet troops returned to Budapest and overthrew the Hungarian Government.)
5 November	British and French paratroops landed at Port Said and Port Fuad.
	U.S.S.R. sent Note to Britain, France and Israel threatening use of force to end intervention. United States rejects as *unthinkable* a Soviet proposal of joint Russian-American intervention in Egypt to stop the fighting.
	Britain and France replied to Secretary-General (Mr Hammarskjold) agreeing to cease all military action as soon as plan for international force to take over from Allies had been accepted by Egypt, and en-endorsed by United Nations.
	Secretary-General informed Britain and France that Israel had accepted unconditional cease-fire, and that in his opinion Egypt had accepted proposed international force.
6 November	Sea-borne assault and landing in Port Said area by Anglo-French force, which had left Malta six days previously. Heavy street fighting in Port Said.
	Prime Minister announced that a cease-fire would be effective from midnight. Anglo-French forces halted at El Cap, 23 miles south of Port Said.
	President Eisenhower re-elected for second term.
7 November	U.N. General Assembly agreed to set up a United Nations police force from non-permanent members of the Security Council. Thirteen nations offered contingents. Sir Anthony Eden announced that 'Allies' would not withdraw until there was a United Nations force *in being* to take over.
12 November	United Nations announced that Egypt had agreed to accept a United Nations force, provided that Egyptian sovereignty was not infringed.
15 November	First contingents of United Nations force arrived in Egypt.
22 December	Evacuation of British troops from Suez completed.
31 December	Clearance work of Canal begun under United Nations auspices after considerable delays imposed by Egyptian Government. (25 March 1957–Canal again clear for big ships.)

SUEZ: TEN YEARS AFTER

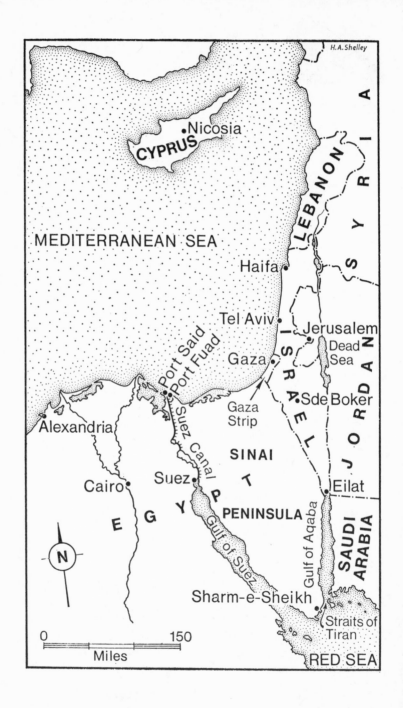

1. Crisis 1956

A documentary by PETER CALVOCORESSI

First broadcast 5 July 1966

OPENING MONTAGE:

Air: One Three from 96 Leader –
Do you think a few of these lights would brighten up
Port Said? After all, it is November the fifth.

Ground: 96 Leader –
A magnificent suggestion
Over

Air: Roger

Air: 82 Make switches . . . Stand by to fire . . . Fire[1]

PETER CALVOCORESSI: Those were noises of war – ground
control chatting with Seahawk pilots over Port Said ten years
ago this November – in the Suez war, in which first Israel and
then Britain and France attacked Nasser's Egypt.

The purpose of this series of broadcasts was to do three
things: to recall the events of that war; to present as much as
possible, as authentically as possible, of the background to the
war and the motives of the participants; and to see where the
participants stand now, ten years later.

This first programme is an introduction and a reminder, a
survey of the war itself and what led up to it. It will be followed
by three programmes also each of an hour's length, by three
shorter programmes on related topics, and finally by an international discussion ranging over the whole of the affair. The
three longer programmes to follow this one will be devoted
to three central topics: first, Egypt – its situation in the fifties,
its politics and aims, its gains and losses from the Suez war;
secondly, a similar programme about Israel. These two – Egypt
and Israel – were the principal Middle Eastern participants in

[1] *BBC Sound Archives.*

the war. But it was not just a Middle Eastern war. The fourth programme will show how and why Britain and France became joined with Israel against Egypt.

This was a war. People got killed. It was a serious episode in the history of all the countries involved. And so I am going to start with the war itself. It lasted one week. It was on 29 October that the Israeli Army crossed its frontiers and attacked Egypt. In a matter of days it overran the Sinai Peninsula – that is to say, the part of Egypt which is east of Suez and so in Asia. The Israelis were helped by the French Air Force, and by the R.A.F., which bombed Egyptian airfields. This campaign was virtually over on 2 November.

On Monday, 5 November, British and French paratroops from Cyprus were dropped in Egypt. On the next day, 6 November, an Anglo-French invasion fleet arrived off Port Said from Malta, where it had been assembling since the summer. But also on that day Britain decided to give up. Still on the same day, the first forerunners of a United Nations force, hastily assembled in less than a week, arrived on the scene, and that was the end of the war.

What were the instructions given to the Commander-in-Chief, at the beginning? Here is an extract from the written despatch of the C-in-C, Allied Forces, General Sir Charles Keightley:

KEIGHTLEY DESPATCH: On 11 August ... I was informed that, in view of Egypt's action in nationalizing the Suez Canal, Her Majesty's Government and the French Government had decided to concentrate certain forces in the Eastern Mediterranean in case armed intervention should be necessary in order to protect their interests and that in this event I was to assume the appointment of Allied Commander-in-Chief of all British and French forces engaged ...

Throughout August and September plans were made to take action in Egypt if some crisis should occur to demand our intervention. These plans were necessarily flexible as it could not be foreseen precisely in what circumstances it might be necessary to intervene.

It may be forgotten ten years later that the Anglo-French operation was a joint one – in every sense of the word. It was conducted by joint staffs, which had been set up three months earlier. The Commander of the French troops, General André Beaufre, explains the set-up and gives his views on its aims and tactics.

ANDRÉ BEAUFRE: For me it began at the beginning of August. My headquarters were many places at the same time. I had a staff in London working with the British. I had a staff in Algiers working with the troops; and I was moving between Algiers, Paris and London. The military objective of the operation was termed: secure the Canal Zone. I do not think that it was really the aim, but it was written that way. I think that this aim really was not, as I said, the real one. The real one was to put out Nasser; but this was not written, and let us say that it was a sort of secret aim. If we were to occupy the Canal Zone and then stay there without any change in the Egyptian Government, I think it would have led to a worse situation than before. The concept of the action was that there should not be an assault landing be-cause the British were very much concerned about casualties; and they wanted to avoid a battle, you see, a real battle for the landing. And, therefore, they had a very funny idea which was to smooth down the Egyptians by a very long so-called psychological phase. That would be achieved by a combin-ation of bombings – destruction of the Egyptian Air Force, and also throwing leaflets and things like that. The plan was to do that for ten days, and after these ten days we were expecting that the Egyptians would wave their hands and say, 'now please come in'. It seemed obvious to me – what happened afterwards – that the world would never let us for ten days do that funny manœuvre, and I objected. They said, 'Yes, but it is the orders.'

In a moment or two I am going back to the origins of the war. But before doing so I want to fill in the events of that crucial war week.

The day after the Israeli attack, Britain and France addressed ultimatums to Israel and Egypt. These threatened Anglo-French intervention in strength, unless both Israel and Egypt ceased hostilities, withdrew ten miles either side of the Suez Canal and allowed an Anglo-French occupation of strategic points along the Canal. Israel accepted the ultimatum conditionally later that same day – Israeli forces were much further away from the Canal than ten miles, and so in effect the ultimatum permitted a further Israeli advance. Egypt rejected the ultimatum – not unnaturally since the cease-fire line, the Suez Canal, was over a hundred miles inside its own territory.

On 2 November, that is after the R.A.F. bombing of Egyptian airfields, the United Nations General Assembly called for a ceasefire and the withdrawal of attacking forces. Egypt accepted these terms on 4 November, Israel did so the following day – after the end of the Sinai campaign. On 6 November – the day the Anglo-French armada reached Port Said – Britain and France also accepted the cease-fire on the understanding that Egypt had agreed to admit an international police force. The reasons for the halting of the operation will emerge before the end of this first programme.

A United Nations' international force was duly dispatched and it stands on the borders between Egypt and Israel to this day.

Briefly, at the United Nations there were three phases: first, after Nasser's nationalization of the Canal Company, the United Nations tried but failed to solve the dispute about how the Canal should be run. Then, the day after the Israeli attack, the Security Council debated a resolution calling for a cease-fire and the withdrawal of Israeli forces; but this resolution was vetoed by France and Britain. Thereupon a special meeting of the full United Nations General Assembly was called, and it adopted a resolution in substantially the same terms. And it was in part to this pressure of world opinion that Britain and France were reacting.

There was also intervention from another quarter. On 5 November, just before the cease-fire, the Soviet Union did two things. It proposed to the United States joint action to stop the Anglo-French operations, and it threatened Britain and France with terrible, if vague, reprisals if they did not desist.

That is what happened. We must now go back and see why it happened. There are two stories to tell. One is the story of the relations between Egypt and Israel. The other is the story of the Aswan Dam and the expropriation by Nasser of the Suez Canal Company.

Israel and Egypt had been in a state of war since 1948, and still were in 1956 – and still are today. The short Arab-Israeli war which followed the establishment of the state of Israel was brought to a stop by armistice agreements but no peace treaties followed. The war went on in a muted way. There were raids across armistice lines in both directions, and Israel was partially blockaded by sea because Egypt prevented the Suez Canal from being used for goods to and from Israel, and also closed the Straits of Tiran which connect the Red Sea with the Gulf of Aqaba and so with the Israeli port of Eilat at the top of that Gulf. An attempt by outside powers to damp down the conflict by arms control was a failure. Both sides got modern weapons, and by 1956, the semi-peace of the preceding six years had become more than usually precarious.

The Aswan Dam is a separate story. I shall go into the questions of the Dam and the Canal in some detail in the next programme on Egypt and the Arab world. Here let me simply recall the salient facts. The Dam was something that Nasser had set his heart on. It was to be the centrepiece of his domestic programme and it seemed that the American and British governments, and the World Bank, were prepared to finance it with certain considerable contributions from Egypt. Then in the middle of July 1956, the Americans went into reverse. A week later, on 26 July, President Nasser retaliated, declaring in a

speech at Alexandria that the Suez Canal Company, which ran
the Canal, was nationalized; and that the Canal revenues would
be used to finance the Dam. This speech fired the train that led
eventually to the Anglo-French attack.

One view is that Nasser reacted to the American decision
on the Dam by nationalizing the Canal Company. Another
view is that Nasser used the decision on the Dam as a pretext
to nationalize the Company. Similarly, one view is that Britain
and France reacted to the nationalization of the Company by
bringing pressure – eventually armed pressure – to bear on
Egypt. Another view is that they used the nationalization of
the Company as a pretext to do what they did.

Here is Sir Anthony Eden's own reaction – from his Ministerial broadcast explaining to the nation why Britain had called
a conference of people interested in the Suez Canal:

EDEN BROADCAST: My friends, we do not seek a solution by
    force, but by the broadest possible international agreement.
    That is why we have called the Conference. We shall do all
    we can to help its work; but this I must make plain. We can-
    not agree that an act of plunder which threatens the liveli-
    hood of many nations shall be allowed to succeed.[1]

One of the most important factors in the situation which
developed between the end of July and the end of October was
a divergence between British and American views. This divergence was, I believe, ultimately to be decisive in stopping the
war, as we shall see later on. On 31 July, President Eisenhower
wrote to the British Prime Minister in these terms:

EISENHOWER LETTER: I have given you my own personal con-
    victions, as well as that of my associates, as to the unwisdom
    even of contemplating the use of military force at this
    moment. Assuming, however, that the whole situation con-
    tinued to deteriorate to the point where such action would
    seem the only recourse, there are certain political facts to

[1] *BBC Sound Archives.*

remember. As you realize, employment of United States forces is possible only through positive action on the part of the Congress, which is now adjourned but can be reconvened on my call for special reasons. If those reasons should involve the issue of employing United States military strength abroad, there would have to be a showing that every peaceful means of resolving the difficulty had previously been exhausted. Without such a showing, there would be a reaction that could very seriously affect our peoples' feeling toward our Western Allies. I do not want to exaggerate, but I assure you that this could grow to such an intensity as to have the most far-reaching consequences.

And here is part of a speech the President made several weeks later. The American attitude was consistent throughout the period and there was no mystery about it. President Eisenhower is commenting on Anglo-French action:

PRESIDENT EISENHOWER: As it is the manifest right of any of the nations to take such decisions and actions, it is likewise our right, if our judgement so dictates, to dissent.

We believe these actions to have been taken in error, for we do not accept that the use of force is a wise or proper instrument for the settlement of international disputes.[1]

Robert Bowie, now a Professor at Harvard and Director of its Center for International Affairs, was an Assistant Secretary of State in the State Department in Washington. When I spoke to him across the Atlantic he explained to me the different British and American attitudes to force after Nasser expropriated the Canal Company.

ROBERT BOWIE: Well, I think basically it was the difference in the way in which Washington and London and also Paris defined the problem. Eisenhower said: we must try to separate the issue of keeping the Canal in operation from the question of the risks from Nasser in other respects, especially

[1] *BBC Sound Archives.*

in the Arab world. This obviously was something which Eden did not accept. He felt the seizure of the Canal was so to speak a first step, and he repeatedly invoked the memory of Hitler and the necessity for dealing with these kinds of things early. He obviously felt that the need was to try to break Nasser, or Nasser's influence, in the area and wished to use this as the occasion. The United States on its side was really trying to focus on how you could assure the safeguarding of the use of the Canal and on mobilizing threats, pressures and so on to bring about some solution which would assure its availability. On the other hand, it seems to me that the French and British attitude was to add to that the question: How can this issue be handled in such a way as to cut down Nasser? Therefore, the efforts of the United States to prolong the negotiations seemed like temporizing to the British and the French, whereas the efforts of the British and the French to bring the thing to a head seemed to be constantly getting in the way of the Eisenhower–Dulles effort to produce an atmosphere in which negotiations might succeed.

I asked Professor Bowie when Washington first warned London against the use of force. He replied by referring to the letter written by President Eisenhower at the end of July (see p. 6).

BOWIE: Well, in that letter Eisenhower said quite clearly that he was concerned at any idea of precipitate use of force, that he felt without any question there must be an exhaustion of all possible peaceful ways to resolve the dispute before even considering the use of force. And he made pretty clear that even then he was not making a conditional commitment but only saying he did not absolutely exclude this as a possibility *in extremis*. But it is quite clear that this must be at the very end of a failure of all other possible means for bringing about peaceful settlement. My own impression is that Dulles always liked to keep in the picture as many risks and threats as possible. I think he would very much have liked to have kept open the possibility as far as Nasser's appraisal went, that if he pushed things too far he might indeed end up with force being used. But it seems to me that his freedom in using this as one instrument for coercing Nasser into a settlement was constantly inhibited because he was fearful as time went on – and I think Eisenhower shared this fear – that if he tried to use this veiled threat then the British and French might use that as a basis for saying the United States had indeed agreed to the use of force.

CALVOCORESSI: If I may interject a comment of my own just for a moment at this point, there is also another distinction, Bowie, between the Anglo-French attitude on force and the American attitude. From the Anglo-French point of view, if you are going to use force, the sooner you use it the better because it becomes more incredible as time has spun out. Whereas in the American view, it was something that, as you say, is not going to be used unless every conceivable alternative has been exhausted and manifestly exhausted and this takes time. So that there was this distinction. Do you agree?

BOWIE: Very much so. I think again this flowed from the somewhat different appraisal as to what was to be the purpose of the use of force. With Eisenhower and Dulles focusing mainly on the question of safeguarding the use of the Canal, the use of force did not seem a particularly sensible way to achieve this. They were fearful that force just would not succeed in accomplishing this aim. First because they feared that it would be extremely difficult to operate the Canal in the face of Egyptian hostility. The Egyptians could so readily sink vessels which would block the Canal, as in fact they did. Also, it would be so easy to sabotage the Canal over a continuing period of time if that was the frame of mind of the Egyptians. Then there was the fear that if war broke out in the Middle East, the pipelines which went through other Arab countries might very well be cut. Again, you remember, that when hostilities broke out, a pipeline, a very major one which went through Syria, was blown up.

The Americans were very fearful of the precedent which would be created, as they saw it, by the precipitate use of force. They were conscious of trying to hold back a number of governments in different parts of the world who felt they too had grievances and who were eager to use force to try to redress them. For example, in South Korea, you may remember, and in Taiwan. The United States probably felt that their restraints would be weakened if in fact they consented to the use of force by France and Britain for redressing what they conceived to be abuses of their interests.

I think the United States was keenly worried by the concern that the use of force by the advanced nations, the former Colonial powers, would create the impression all through the less developed world, including South Asia and Africa and Latin America, that there was a sort of return to an attitude of domination or neo-Colonialist attitude. Now I am not suggesting for a minute there are not partial answers to each of these points. I am trying to describe what I think was in the minds of Eisenhower and Dulles as factors in the decision.

26 July to 29 October is a long time. What was going on between Nasser's Alexandria speech and the actual attack on Egypt? There were, first of all, international discussions about the running of the Canal. Britain and France took the lead in trying to assert international control through diplomacy. At the same time they were building up powerful forces in the Mediterranean. Their motives for so doing we will examine later. It suffices to say here that during August, September and October there were many who suspected that the British and French governments were aiming at something more than a new international régime for the Canal, namely the fall of the Nasser régime itself. These fears prompted attempts at the United Nations to arrange a peaceful settlement between Egypt

and Britain and France, and these negotiations, too, ran parallel
with separate and for the most part secret Anglo-French
confabulations and military dispositions. To recall the events
of these three months and assess their significance, I spoke to
Thomas Barman, who observed the various conferences and
manœuvrings from London where he was Diplomatic Cor-
respondent of the BBC.

THOMAS BARMAN: The first thing was, I think, that the Americans became alarmed, perhaps puzzled is the better word, at the
anger shown in London and Paris over the nationalization
of the Canal. Dulles was away – a long way away from
Washington – and the man in charge of the State Department,
Mr Murphy, was sent over to London by the President and
he arrived here on 28 July. He was immediately seen by
Mr Macmillan, who invited him to dinner. Now Macmillan
told Murphy that what the British Government proposed to
do was to land a division or two in Egypt. It would all be
over in ten days. They would then have disposed of Nasser,
and the Government had in fact set aside five million pounds
for this purpose. Dulles then came over to find out whether
the facts as reported by Murphy really were so. He spent the
whole day in conference with Selwyn Lloyd, and Pineau and
the result of those talks was an agreement to summon an
international conference of the powers principally concerned,
principally interested in the Suez Canal. It included all those
who signed the 1888 convention, plus the Maritime powers.
CALVOCORESSI: This conference actually met in London on
16 August. What was its object?
BARMAN: The object of that conference was to see if they could
restore the Suez Canal to international control. I want to
make an important point here: the British and French governments were concerned to re-establish the ownership to the
Canal, their ownership; the other powers, and principally
the United States, were concerned to maintain freedom of
navigation through the Canal, which was a totally different

idea. Nevertheless the conference, including the United States, did agree to put forward a plan for putting the Canal under international control, on which Egypt would be represented, but nevertheless under international control with an administrator who would be reporting regularly to the United Nations.

CALVOCORESSI: If I heard you correctly, I think you said a moment ago that the British and French were concerned to re-establish their ownership over the Canal. Is that right? Had they ever had ownership and were they not concerned to establish ownership and, therefore, to assert something which did not exist, either in the 1888 convention or in the concession. They were asking for something new.

BARMAN: I think that is correct.

CALVOCORESSI: There was really a basic misunderstanding, was there not at the heart of the conference, because there were those who believed that the efficient running of the Canal was something that was beyond the Egyptians' powers, that this was a technical matter which Egyptians simply could not encompass. On the other hand I know the Norwegians, for instance, said at the conference that the running of the Canal was not nearly as difficult as some people made out and that in any case the Egyptians were perfectly competent to do so – and there were others who said the same thing. In fact, this judgement of the Norwegians, and others, turned out to be correct.

BARMAN: There were other problems involved, problems which were peculiar to this country and to the French. In the first place there were frantic appeals for help from Nuri Pasha in Baghdad to the British Government. And he made the point that, unless Nasser was tamed and kept in order, the régime in Iraq could not last. I think this was a very important factor in British policy. From the French point of view what was at stake was Algeria. These two governments had these two separate purposes in mind, over and above the Suez Canal.

CALVOCORESSI: And these other purposes were not, of course, on the agenda of this conference.

BARMAN: They had nothing whatever to do with the conference. People suspected there were these motives; and that, of course, added to the suspicions in Washington, and I should say in the Scandinavian states.

CALVOCORESSI: Now the outcome of the August conference was a mission to Cairo.

BARMAN: Yes. The August conference, of course, did not speak with one voice. Twenty-three or -four governments were represented, but they did not agree on the final proposals that emerged. Those proposals were accepted only by eighteen, and were then taken to Cairo by Mr Menzies (the Australian Prime Minister) for discussion, for presentation to President Nasser.

CALVOCORESSI: And these proposals amounted to what?

BARMAN: They were in very general terms. They began by saying that the eighteen wanted the Canal to be efficiently operated, that the Canal had to be insulated from the politics of any one nation and that the Canal should yield a fair return to Egypt. They wanted the Canal to be operated by an international board of directors responsible for maintaining, operating and developing the Canal – that is to say outside Egyptian control though, of course, there would be an Egyptian on the board – and that this board would eventually report to the United Nations. But it did mean taking the Canal out of Egyptian sovereign control.

CALVOCORESSI: And in any case as, we know, the mission ended in failure; and I think it is relevant to point out that on the very next day, on the 10 September, the French Prime Minister and Foreign Minister, Mollet and Pineau, arrived in London for talks with their British opposite numbers. So you get the switch which you keep getting throughout these months I think, from international discussion to Anglo-French discussion.

BARMAN: Yes, you got that the whole time. I think one of the factors here was that when the French felt we were getting too close to the Americans, that is to say when Sir Anthony Eden was trying to adjust his policy to be more acceptable to Washington, he really was on the point of betraying the French.

CALVOCORESSI: There was then a further attempt at international accord of some kind?

BARMAN: Yes, there was a second conference in the middle of September; and this was a conference which sought to establish a Suez Canal Users' Association [SCUA]. The idea was that the Canal Users' Association should appoint their own pilots. They should organize their own convoys through the Canal and the Canal dues should be paid direct to them and not to the Egyptians.

CALVOCORESSI: And it broke down on this question of dues?

BARMAN: The United States Government had not the power to compel American ship owners to pay Canal dues to anybody. That is to say if the American ship owners decided to pay their dues to the Egyptians that was their business. They could not be forced to pay them to SCUA. So in the event pretty well the only people who paid to the Association were British ship owners and, therefore, the scheme did not work.

CALVOCORESSI: So having failed at this point to get a scheme adopted by an *ad hoc* conference of Maritime powers, the British and French then moved to try and get a more, what shall I say, formal or legal endorsement of their plans from the United Nations.

BARMAN: Yes, I think that they took it to the United Nations in the hope that, if they got a Security Council resolution enforcing the establishment of SCUA with all its consequences, they would be immeasurably strengthened and that they would then have moral authority, if you like, for doing what they liked in fighting their way, shooting their way through the Canal if necessary. In the event, of course, the Security Council after very long debates would not play and the resolution was vetoed by the Soviet Union.

CALVOCORESSI: Then again, at the end of the Security Council debate, we see the same pattern reasserting itself, the resumption of the Anglo-French dialogue, because within a couple of days of the end of that debate Eden and Lloyd go to Paris for meetings with Mollet and Pineau.

BARMAN: The French were determined so far as it was in their power to keep the British up to the mark. The French had made up their minds – they were going all the way. They were not sure the British would.

In the last ten days of October the die was cast for war and against peace. These ten days contain what has been the biggest mystery of the Suez affair – the issue called collusion. At that time British Ministers denied collusion between Britain and Israel. French and Israeli personages on the other hand have done the opposite. We shall come to this in our fourth programme, where, among other things, we shall examine the evidence about a secret meeting outside Paris towards the end of October, attended by Ben-Gurion himself and by senior French and British Ministers – and the signing of a secret 'treaty' on behalf of all three governments.

We have come back to the eve of the war. Let me recapitulate. The Israelis attacked on 29 October, and were victorious in less than a week. On Monday 5 November, when the Israeli campaign was over, the Anglo-French parachutists went in.

Meanwhile on the day before, Sunday 4 November, at dawn, a dramatic broadcast sounded from a completely different quarter.

IMRE NAGY: This is Imre Nagy, Chairman of the Council of Ministers of the Hungarian People's Republic speaking. In the early hours of the morning Soviet troops have started an attack against the Hungarian capital with the apparent purpose of overthrowing the lawful democratic government of the country. Our troops are engaged in battle. The government is in its place. This is my message to the Hungarian people and to the whole world.[1]

A few hours later came an urgent and moving appeal from Radio Rakoczi – in English.

RADIO RAKOCZI: This is Hungary calling. This is Hungary calling. Early this morning the Soviet troops launched a general attack on Hungary. We are requesting you to send us immediate aid in the form of parachute troops over the Transdanubian provinces. . . . For the sake of God and freedom, help Hungary![2]

One of the later programmes[3] in this series will be a talk about the Hungarian rising and its impact – if any – on Suez, or vice versa. I have included these extracts from Hungarian broadcasts, because the emotional impact in this country of the events in Budapest was considerable, and contributed greatly to the sometimes hysterical atmosphere which surrounded the Suez crisis in these days.

It was anyhow necessary to re-explain British policy and the Prime Minister and the Foreign Secretary did so in Parliament and by broadcasting. They claimed that they had suddenly been faced with a highly inflammable situation in the Middle East and had decided to plunge in to prevent it getting worse. This was the Prime Minister:

EDEN BROADCAST: In the depths of our conviction we decided that here was the beginning of a forest fire, of immense danger to peace. We decided that we must act and act quickly.

What should we do? We put the matter to the Security Council. Should we have left it to them? Should we have been content to wait to see whether they would act? How long would this have taken? And where would the forest fire have spread in the meantime? Would words have been enough?

---

[1] BBC Sound Archives; broadcast in Hungarian.
[2] BBC Sound Archives.   [3] Programme VI.

What we did do, was to take police action at once. Action to end the fighting and to separate the armies. . . .

We have stepped in because the United Nations could not do so in time.[1]

And the Foreign Secretary, Selwyn Lloyd, a few days later:

LLOYD BROADCAST: Late on 29 October, Israeli forces crossed the border and appeared to be sweeping the Egyptian Army before them. They pushed detachments forwards towards the Suez Canal and by the morning of 30 October we had to face the prospect not only of war spreading through the Middle East, but also the probability that one of the battle grounds would be the area of the Suez Canal. In or near the Canal at that time there were many British ships, British merchant seamen and other British subjects about their lawful occasions.

The British and French governments decided to take speedy action and to request both sides to stop hostilities, to withdraw ten miles from the area of the Canal, and to permit Anglo-French detachments to be stationed in Port Said, Ismailia, and Suez as guarantors of peace.

We wished as rapidly as possible to put a protective shield between the combatants, to prevent hostilities and to try to stop the war spreading.[2]

The Leader of the Opposition, claiming the right to reply to the Prime Minister's broadcast, saw things differently. Mr Gaitskell said that having rejected the United Nations resolution we had gone to war with Egypt. He went on:

GAITSKELL BROADCAST: Why was it done? The Prime Minister justifies it on these grounds: first of all, he says, to protect British lives and property. But there has been no rescue operation. Instead, to tell the truth, thousands of British civilians now living in Egypt have been put in grave danger, because of what we have done.

[1] *BBC Sound Archives.*   [2] *BBC Sound Archives.*

B

The Prime Minister says it was to safeguard the Canal and the free passage through it. What has happened to the Canal? It is blocked because of what we have done. Was the Canal indeed ever really menaced before we began bombing? I very much doubt it. There is no evidence to show that it was.

I am afraid the real reason for going to war with Egypt was different. I have seen the text of the first broadcast of Allied Command to the Egyptians. This is what it said, in Arabic of course. 'O Egyptians, why has this befallen you? First because Abdul Nasser went mad and seized the Suez Canal.' The broadcast was right. It was this which really induced the Prime Minister to decide on invasion.

The Prime Minister has said we were going in to separate the two sides, but you do not separate two armies by bombing airfields and landing troops a hundred miles behind one side only. No, this is a second onslaught on a country which was already the victim of an attack.

Now a new idea has been put forward. The idea that we are going in to make way for a United Nations force. But nothing was said about this in the Ultimatum to Egypt. Nothing was said about this at the Security Council. If this was the Government's plan, why on earth did they not put it forward before?[1]

In what remains of this programme we shall concentrate on what has always seemed to me the cardinal issue of why Britain, having invaded Egypt on a Monday, decided to call off the operation on Tuesday. But before embarking on this inquiry, let me tell you that two of the points which may have been raised in your minds by those Ministerial statements you just heard will be taken up in two later programmes in the series. Mr Herbert Nicholas of New College, Oxford, will be giving a talk[2] on United Nations intervention, and particularly on the effect of Suez on the development of the United Nations peace-keeping functions. And for the constitutional echoes in

[1] *BBC Sound Archives.*   [2] *Programme VII.*

this country we shall be hearing from a political biographer, Mr Robert Rhodes James.[1]

Now, for the ending of the affair. There is no dispute about who cried halt. It was the British. The French were forced to react to a definite British decision to stop. There were a number of ingredients in this decision. The principal ones – and I am not now trying to put them in any order of importance – were American attitudes, Commonwealth attitudes, the Russian threats, British public opinion and the Prime Minister's health. We cannot enlarge on this last point because we do not know enough about it. We will begin with public opinion. We went to Dr Henry Durant, the man who knows most about it from having directed the Gallup Poll in Britain for thirty years. I asked Dr Durant if he could confirm that the Suez crisis created the bitter split in public opinion in this country it was believed to have done.

HENRY DURANT: Absolutely correct, yes. If you look at the results from the polls we were taking at that time, you would find this kind of picture: we asked 'do you agree or disagree with the way Eden has handled the Middle East situation?' and we found eighty-nine per cent of the Conservatives supporting him. Now his party was almost solidly behind him. But we found sixty-three per cent of the Labour Party, two in three of every Labour Party supporter, opposed to Eden. You see, that is a very sharp split indeed.

CALVOCORESSI: And when you put these figures together, disregarding party affiliations, what sort of picture do you get?

DURANT: The majority, fifty-three per cent, was supporting Eden, and this is one of the interesting things that came out all the time from our polls. Eden was supported by the majority of the people with regards to his general policy.

CALVOCORESSI: So he had a majority, but it was a majority that was not far above fifty. What about attitudes to force?

[1] Programme V.

When did people first become aware of the possibility that force might be used and what did they think about it?

DURANT: I think it was when the reservists were called up in late September that people first became aware of the possibility of using force. A big majority, two in three, thought it was the proper precaution to take. But when trouble really developed and there was fighting, we never found a majority of the public saying that they approved of Britain taking military action. The proportion favouring military action hovered somewhere between forty and fifty per cent, but never reached fifty per cent.

CALVOCORESSI: When the action was called off abruptly, did you do any research into whether people thought that having got as far as that we ought to have gone on?

DURANT: Yes, we asked them what should Britain and France have done when there was the call for the cease-fire; and only one in three said we should have gone on. The majority, fifty-three per cent, said it was perfectly correct to stop.

CALVOCORESSI: So they accepted a sort of international thumbs down verdict! Do you know why they did this?

DURANT: You remember the call was made in the name of the United Nations. One of the things that has come out very clearly since the war is that the public want the United Nations to take action. I would judge that the main reason for wanting to stop is that most of the world was ranged against us.

Now the Russian threats, and here there are two questions. There is the question whether the Russian threats had, in fact, any effect on the British Cabinet's decision on 6 November, to accept a cease-fire; and there is also the question whether the Russians were themselves serious, or were merely bluffing. On this point of Russian intentions and Russian capabilities, here are the views of John Erickson, a Senior Lecturer at Manchester University and the leading historian in this country on Russian military affairs. We have to distinguish between the threat to send volunteers to the Middle East and the threat to use missiles against London and Paris. Dr Erickson remarks first on the volunteers:

JOHN ERICKSON: The first mention ever made of volunteers was by Mr Khrushchev at the Rumanian Embassy on 23 August 1956, though this was not reported in the Soviet Press. It was taken up only by Egyptian newspapers. Incidentally at about this time came the offer of Communist Chinese volunteers. Now the only actual reference to volunteers in the Soviet Press, which would enable Soviet readers and presumably potential volunteers to read it, was on 6 November, that is the day of the cease-fire. And only four days later, that is on 10 November, when fighting was clearly over, did TASS, the Soviet News Agency, announce that the Soviet Government will not hinder – that is it would allow – the dispatch of volunteers, and volunteers to a war which, of course, had long since ceased to exist.

CALVOCORESSI: There is the more serious matter of missiles. When was the missile threat made; and just what did the Russians threaten?

ERICKSON: Well, we might look at this very quickly in terms of what the Russians had done from 1 November. The first Russian intervention in the international crisis was a suggestion that there should be an intervention by the Bandung powers, an appeal by the Soviet President to President Nehru and President Sukarno. And then between the third and fourth of November there was a silence because the Russians were busy with Hungary. Then on the evening of 5 November, Moscow broadcast the text of a note to the British Ambassador, a text pointing out that this Anglo-French activity must cease and that threats could be levelled – and this is what the Russians said – 'by other means', other than navies and air forces, that is by rockets, against Britain and France. Now at the same time Marshal Bulganin communicated with President Eisenhower that both the Soviet

Union and the United States should in combination – and this is a quote – 'curb aggression' in the Middle East, and what was specifically mentioned this time was a co-operation with the American Sixth Fleet.

CALVOCORESSI: Can I just recapitulate at this point? These are two separate things that happened on 5 November. Am I right in saying that at this point the Hungarian situation was under control?

ERICKSON: Yes. The Russians had obtained clearly their first objectives in Hungary, and had the situation in hand.

CALVOCORESSI: So on that day the Russians did two things. They addressed notes to Britain and France in slightly different terms which were of a threatening nature. And they also approached Washington and said 'Let us do something together.'

ERICKSON: That is right. They made two distinct interventions: one of a threatening nature, the other of a co-operative nature with the United States. And the next stage in the proceedings, of course, is at 1.00 a.m. on the morning of 6 November, when the Soviet representative at the United Nations repeated the Soviet request for United States and Soviet intervention if both Great Britain and France did not cease their aggressive operations against Egypt.

CALVOCORESSI: And the American reply was?

ERICKSON: To reject the Soviet suggestion and to counter threaten, that is to pose an entirely new threat, that if the Russians unloosed their rockets against Britain and France, then they would have to face American retaliation. Now it was this American counter threat which clearly took the sting and indeed took the timing out of the Soviet ultimatum which was allowed to die a small little death and was never heard of again.

CALVOCORESSI: Now supposing, for the sake of the argument, the Russians had really intended to do something at this point, had they the capacity?

ERICKSON: They had, of course, only a fractional intercontinental capability; and at that time the balance of the strength was with the Americans. Now let us talk about what they could have done against France and Britain. Yes, if it is true they had their first-generation ground to ground missiles which were modified V2 type German rockets with a limited range. They could presumably have fired some rockets, presumably at certain targets but this would have been by and large, I would submit, a sporadic and unco-ordinated operation.

CALVOCORESSI: The range being something like three to four hundred miles?

ERICKSON: Assuming that the Russians were able to launch these rockets from the western extremities of their *bloc* (at a time when the Communist *bloc* was itself in an uproar, thus scarcely providing the ideal base from which to mount a 'rocket attack'), even with this deployment the T-1 (M 101), quantity-produced since the early 1950s, a modified V-2 single-stage, liquid-fuelled tactical attack missile with its 800 lb. nuclear warhead but with a range of only 400–450 miles, could scarcely bring London under threat. There was certainly in existence an intermediate range ballistic missile, the IRBM T-2 (M 103), a two-stage, liquid-fuelled vehicle with a 700 lb. nuclear warhead which had been range-tested over 1,000 miles (effective range 800–1,100 miles) but during the years 1955–56 this missile had been in small-scale pro-duction only and was thus not operationally deployed in any strength (serial production began only in 1957). It was a far cry, in terms of a really credible threat, from the missile firing-range to 'missile bombardment' such as Khrushchev suggested.

CALVOCORESSI: This would be an attack directed westwards. What about the possibility of attack directed on Cyprus where there was a British force after all rather inadequately protected?

ERICKSON: This again would have been a possibility but as far as I can discover there was simply no evidence whatsoever of the movement of long-range Russian aircraft capable of this kind of mission, although – and this is important – the Russian air force and military establishment were on full alert because of the Hungarian and Polish situation.

If Dr Erickson is right, as I feel sure he is, the British Cabinet did not have to worry about the Russian threats – except in a minor way. It would be concerned, I imagine, to avoid giving the slightest impression that it was influenced by them. So far as Arab opinion was concerned this was difficult, perhaps impossible, and the Russians did score a propaganda victory in the Arab world. Elsewhere I doubt if they did.

The Americans played an altogether different and much more significant role. Two witnesses whom I will now call agreed that the American attitude – financial and political – was decisive, although they put it differently.

The first of these witnesses is Paul Bareau. He has been writing on economic affairs, national and international, since before the second world war. At the time of Suez he was City Editor of the *News Chronicle* and at the present time he is Editor-in-Chief of the *Statist*. I asked Mr Bareau if the crucial reason for the halt on 6 November, was financial.

PAUL BAREAU: I think the crucial reason was much more political. But we were in an extremely difficult financial situation. The crisis which affected sterling in 1956 was the most serious which had occurred over the post-war years. I should like to add though that the underlying position of sterling at that time was extremely sound. We had a balance of payments surplus in 1956, and, therefore, the pressure on sterling was entirely a question of confidence. It was emotional. It was caused by a withdrawal of funds by all kinds of other countries.

CALVOCORESSI: Can you quantify this a bit? I think it was generally said at that time that there was a sort of plimsoll line for sterling, if I may so put it, around about two thousand million. Were we well above that?

BAREAU: Yes, two thousand million dollars was about the plimsoll line. At the beginning of the crisis I think we were in the region of two thousand eight hundred million dollars and it came down in the last four months of 1956 to two thousand four hundred million dollars.

CALVOCORESSI: If we take an arbitrary date – say 1 November – the position at that time was not that we were broke. The trouble was that one did not know how much more one was going to lose. Is that right?

BAREAU: That is quite right. And, of course, a country like Britain can lose a great deal of gold because we are international bankers. We hold reserve balances for a large number of other countries, and they are at complete liberty to exchange the sterling balances into gold or into other currencies. And that, in fact, is what had been happening. The countries which were drawing down sterling balances included India. She was at the beginning of her second five-year plan. She knew she would have to pay for imports of capital goods, and taking a rather dim view of sterling, she took sterling away and paid for these goods in advance while the going was good. Another rather interesting example was China. She had a good deal of sterling, converted part of that sterling into Swiss francs and put the Swiss francs at the disposal of Egypt.

CALVOCORESSI: Who were the other large depositors who were expected to take their money away?

BAREAU: Among the largest were the Middle East oil states, who did begin to take sterling away. They keep a considerable amount of sterling here.

CALVOCORESSI: Did they begin to do this when the fighting started, or when the crisis started way back in July?

BAREAU: The main drawing from that quarter occurred after the fighting started. And I believe this would have continued even if we had succeeded in the Suez episode.

CALVOCORESSI: For political reasons?

BAREAU: For political reasons, yes.

CALVOCORESSI: Given the rate of loss in the last week, shall we say, before the operation was stopped, how long financially speaking could we have gone on?

BAREAU: I think we could have gone on for another six to eight weeks. Certainly after that the plimsoll line would have been broken and we would have been faced with a serious problem.

CALVOCORESSI: This means you have got to devalue your currency. And apart from this there was no other reason why one could conceivably want to devalue sterling at this particular time?

BAREAU: None at all. We were not in the fundamental disequilibrium. We would not, therefore, have had any case to present to the International Monetary Fund and ask for the devaluation of sterling.

CALVOCORESSI: So we would have been forced to devalue sterling if we had gone on to these six to eight weeks, when there was no other reason for doing it at all, no financial one.

BAREAU: That is right. Quite right.

CALVOCORESSI: Now, you mentioned the International Monetary Fund, the I.M.F. We did, in fact, go to the I.M.F. and we did, in fact, get money from elsewhere, did we not?

BAREAU: Yes. The main rescue operation occurred after we stopped fighting. This was in December 1956. We borrowed all that we could take from the International Monetary Fund, which was one thousand three hundred million dollars. We also borrowed five hundred million dollars from the Export-Import Bank in Washington. That was to pay for commodities which we had to buy in the United States, particularly for oil.

CALVOCORESSI: That is, in effect, American Government money.

BAREAU: It is American Government money which can only be used in order to pay for imports from the United States.

CALVOCORESSI: Was it a condition of the rescue operation that the fighting should stop?

BAREAU: Well, I was not privy to the negotiations but I am quite sure that if the fighting had continued we would certainly not have got the five hundred million dollar Export-Import Bank loan, which is United States Government money; and I doubt whether we would have got International Monetary Fund credits, because the United States vote on that organization is a fairly decisive one.

CALVOCORESSI: So we come back to the point where this is an element of decisive American intervention.

BAREAU: Yes.

In discussion with Monty Woodhouse I asked his views on a whole range of factors affecting the British decision to stop, and we then went on to consider the effect of the Suez war on Britain's Middle East position and on President Nasser's standing too. Mr Woodhouse is the author of a number of books on an enviable range of subjects including one on British foreign policy since the war. In 1956 he was Director-General of the Royal Institute of International Affairs, Chatham House. When he left Chatham House it was in order to go into politics, and after a brief stay on the back benches he held junior office in the Macmillan and Home administrations. I asked him his views on why Britain pulled out of the Suez operation so abruptly.

C. M. WOODHOUSE: The run on sterling has always seemed to me to be the decisive factor; and the obvious reluctance of the Americans to help us to stem the run on sterling so long as the operation was going on.

CALVOCORESSI: What about the personal pressures brought to bear by people like Eisenhower?

WOODHOUSE: I think that Eisenhower personally probably did not have a very great impact. He was known to be a very upright and pro-British figure. But I am sure the dominant man in American politics at that time was Dulles and there was a really very unhappy relation between Dulles and Eden which went back to the Far East crisis of 1954.

CALVOCORESSI: But I suppose it is true to say that British Ministers cared in general about American opinion? We had a close and sensitive association with the Americans which the French did not have. The French have probably discounted American opposition already.

WOODHOUSE: That is perfectly true. I think the French were in a position to be more independent of American opinion.

CALVOCORESSI: What about the Commonwealth?

WOODHOUSE: At the overt levels they were all against us except Australia and New Zealand. But I am pretty sure from my reading of events at the time that this had been discounted in advance by the British government. In other words they knew how Commonwealth opinion was going to manifest itself, and this I think is fundamentally the reason why they did not consult the Commonwealth governments before taking the action. After all, if you know your friends are going to advise you not to do what you have already decided to do, it is not much service to anybody to ask them for their opinion.

CALVOCORESSI: And we have to remember that the number of members of the Commonwealth in 1956 was still moderate.

WOODHOUSE: This, of course, is true. There were no African members.

CALVOCORESSI: One of the more curious and I suppose one can say disturbing aspects of the whole affair was the length of time it took from the decision to take action to the time when the action was actually taken, the preparations were very long drawn out from the last week in July till the first day of November roughly speaking. Why was this, and what was the decisive point in this process?

WOODHOUSE: It was a sign of a grave weakness in our defence policy in the preceding years. This, of course, was why there was a tremendous shake up of defence policy with the Sandys White Paper in the following year. The decisive moment in the build-up of the operation always seemed to me at the time to be the decision to call up reservists, specialist reservists, without whom it was impossible to mount the operation. This was a sign in itself of the weakness of our defence policy, that we could not even mount such a comparatively small operation without calling up reservists. But once they were called up, then the government was on a slippery slope: if you call up reservists you have either got to use them or let them go home. Once you let them go home, that would have been equivalent to conceding victory to President Nasser. Therefore, it has always seemed to me – and it seemed to me at the time – that the moment the reservists had to be called up, the government had tied its own hands and was inevitably committed to some kind of action.

Finally I asked Mr Woodhouse how he thought the operation had affected our position in the Middle East.

WOODHOUSE: Well, I think that what happened at the end of 1956, was what you might call a process of catalysis. It was not so much that anything changed in our position in the Middle East, because our position in the Middle East had already crumbled away. For years before 1956 we no longer had any power in the Middle East. What the Suez fiasco did was to demonstrate this fact, that we had no power. It merely brought to light something that was already the case and forced everyone to recognize it. One respect in which there was a change in our relative position in the Middle East is that, of course, Suez ended up as a resounding success for Nasser. Instead of precipitating his downfall, as was no doubt the intention, it gave him a tremendous moral victory, which he has been living off ever since.

A resounding success for Nasser? True perhaps in 1956. I am less sure if his credit balance is so strong today in Egypt or the Arab world. Anyway in our next programme President Nasser himself explains some of the problems in an interview specially recorded for this series.

I have aimed so far to remind you of the events which took us into the shortest war in our history, and to give some assessment of why it was so short. In this war our ally was France, the unacknowledged ally Israel, the enemy Egypt. Why Egypt?

2. Egyptian Outlook

A documentary by PETER CALVOCORESSI

First broadcast 7 July 1966

PETER CALVOCORESSI: This second programme is about Egypt. It will be followed by a parallel programme about Israel. For this programme President Nasser has – for the first time – recorded his views about the Suez war; and in the Israeli programme you will hear Mr Ben-Gurion and other Israeli leaders.

I must begin by spending a few minutes on the relations between Egypt and Israel, and between Egypt and Britain, in the period before the Suez war.

When Israel came into existence it survived an Arab attempt to kill it at birth. For the Arabs, Israel then became a problem which was better postponed. They had lost this war against Israel because they were disunited and inefficient. Defeat rankled. Many groups, ashamed of what had happened, put the blame on the rulers and decided to get rid of them as a first step to efficiency and unity.

So the Israeli war was a spur to revolutions in the Arab world which were already cooking for other reasons. Syria soon experienced the first of a chain of coups. Abdullah of Jordan was murdered. Most important, in 1952 a group of young officers overthrew the Egyptian monarchy.

But these revolutions did not usher in Arab unity. Some anti-revolutionary régimes survived – in Iraq until 1958; in Saudi Arabia until today. New governments tended to be ranged against older and more conservative ones. Nor did the new men exactly rush into each other's arms. If Arab unity meant accepting the leadership of Egypt, there were a number of modernists outside Egypt who hesitated. The Arab world remained divided, and therefore weak, and therefore suspicious.

The Arabs were suspicious not only of each other but also of outsiders. This was especially true of the British who were more in evidence than other outsiders and were the sole survivors of the age when Arabs had had to put up with foreign rule – Turkish rule, and then British and French. And none were more suspicious of the British than the Egyptians whose country had been dominated and occupied by the British since 1881, and who made it a point of pride to get the British out of the Suez Canal Zone and out of the Sudan.

Middle Eastern politics were complicated by the criss-crossing of these two major forces: anti-British feeling; and the division of the Arab world into modernizing republics and conservative monarchies. The British were regarded by the new men as the friends of the old lot and so indeed they were. But to men like Colonel Nasser Britain's friendship with, for example, the Iraqi dynasty and its semi-perpetual Prime Minister, Nuri Pasha, was not only regrettable but positively sinister. The British, it seemed to Nasser, were ganging up with the forces of reaction to defeat the forces of progress, and to perpetuate British influence in the Middle East.

Egypt is much the most important of the Arab countries. Britain was still in the early fifties the most important of the outside powers which were active in the Middle East. Soon after the Egyptian revolution in 1952, Egypt and Britain made a real effort to get on good terms. The British agreed to evacuate the Canal Zone and to leave the Sudan. True, the British retained a number of other strong points in the Arab world (like Aden) but the specifically *Egyptian* points of friction were to be eliminated.

Then, almost in the same breath, things began to go wrong. By the early fifties the Cold War had crept into the Middle East and the principal Western powers were looking for a way of creating an anti-Russian alliance of themselves and as many Middle Eastern states as could be persuaded to join them. The leading candidates in Western minds were Turkey and Iran – plus Pakistan – all of them non-Arab states. But then the

British – for special reasons of their own – pressed for the addition of Iraq and Jordan, and immediately every Egyptian suspicion was aroused. For Iraq and Jordan were two monarchies under related kings of the Hashemite line, the focus of Arab opposition to Nasser and all he stood for. To Nasser this new alliance, called the Baghdad Pact after Iraq joined, was a conspiracy between Imperial Britain and Arab reactionaries. Nasser denounced the pact, the British and the Hashemites. He prevented Jordan from joining it, and later the King of Jordan found himself forced to get rid of his British Commander-in-Chief, General Glubb. A regular Anglo-Egyptian hate was under-way. The good intentions of 1954 vanished in misunderstanding and distrust.

A few weeks ago in Cairo, Erskine Childers asked President Nasser to cast his mind back to the period of honeymoon and rupture.

PRESIDENT NASSER: We hoped, after a long period of British occupation and domination which lasted about eighty years, to begin new relations based on equality and respect.

ERSKINE CHILDERS: Did you expect that there would be a change in the British policy of trying to make strategic alliances?

NASSER: We expected that there would be no attempts to bring Arab countries into any pact other than the Arab Collective Security Pact.[1]

CHILDERS: In December 1955 when General Templer went to Jordan to try to get Jordan to join the Baghdad Pact you made a very strong reaction over Cairo radio and in the newspapers. Why was this in particular?

NASSER: First of all, in April, before going to Bandung I got a promise through the ambassador here from Mr Eden that Britain would not try by any means to have any other Arab

[1] Drawn up by the Arab League Council in 1950 and ratified between 1951 and 1953 by Egypt, Iraq, Jordan, Lebanon, Saudi Arabia, Syria, and Yemen [Childers].

country joining the Baghdad Pact. Then suddenly came this Templer mission trying to persuade Jordan to be a member of the Baghdad Pact. That is why our reaction was very hard.

CHILDERS: I think some people in the British Government thought that you were responsible for the ousting of Glubb Pasha in Jordan, and that you made a point of telling Mr Selwyn Lloyd this when he was here at dinner with you. What was the truth about all that?

NASSER: Mr Selwyn Lloyd was taking dinner with me that night, and he got the message during the dinner. I got the message after arriving home that Glubb had been expelled from the Jordanian Army. Mr Selwyn Lloyd was to pass by about eight o'clock in the morning the next day, on his way to the aerodrome. I was not yet getting full information about the whole story of Glubb, and I thought that this was a move by the British Government. And to my understanding this was a very good move and a very progressive move, because Glubb was aggravating the hatred of the Arabs in Jordan against Britain. So, when I saw Mr Selwyn Lloyd next morning I told him: congratulations about this step. He thought that I was joking, about him. But I thought that this step was taken by the British Government. The reaction of Mr Selwyn Lloyd was nervous, and I was surprised about his nervousness. Then he left without telling me anything. After that I received information about the whole story, and I realized why Mr Selwyn Lloyd was nervous.

It was partly as a result of incidents like this that British Ministers formed an extremely hostile picture of Nasser. Sir Anthony Eden, broadcasting as Prime Minister, expressed his view:

EDEN BROADCAST: Some people say 'Colonel Nasser's promised not to interfere with shipping passing through the Canal. Why, therefore, don't we trust him?' Well, the answer is simple. Look at his record. Our quarrel is not with Egypt – still less with the Arab world; it is with Colonel Nasser . . .

He told us that he wanted a new spirit of Anglo-Egyptian relations. We welcomed that, but instead of meeting us with friendship Colonel Nasser conducted a vicious propaganda campaign against our country. He has shown that he is not a man who can be trusted to keep an agreement . . .

We all know this is how Fascist governments behave and we all remember, only too well, what the cost can be in giving in to Fascism.[1]

In Paris, opinions were divided. The Prime Minister, Guy Mollet, was inclined to go some way with Eden but the Foreign Minister, Christian Pineau, who had met Nasser earlier in the year, was less hostile:

CHRISTIAN PINEAU: We were anxious, and particularly my friend Guy Mollet, of the ideas of Nasser about the domination of the Arab people. We read at this period Nasser's book on the principles of revolution, and in the mind of Guy Mollet it was the relation between this book and Hitler's *Mein Kampf*.

CALVOCORESSI: When Nasser expropriated the Suez Canal Company, you formed certain conclusions about the consequences of this. Now, in forming these conclusions you presumably were guided to some extent by your own personal contacts with Nasser. You were in Cairo in March 1956. What impressions did you get of Nasser during your time there and immediately afterwards?

PINEAU: Not so bad as you might think, because when I came back from Cairo I said to Guy Mollet: I think sincerely that Nasser is not a second Hitler . . .

CALVOCORESSI: . . . is *not* . . .

PINEAU: . . . Is not. He is not a second Hitler. He is a man without big political experience, and I am sure that he will never be the dictator of the Middle East. But Guy Mollet was not so sure as me of this impression.

CALVOCORESSI: Looking at this ten years later, do you think

[1] *BBC Sound Archives.*

you were right in March 1956, or do you think the other people were right about Nasser's character?

PINEAU: Ten years after, my opinion is the same about Nasser.

The comparison between Nasser and Hitler haunted many people of Hitler's generation. Looking back, André Fontaine, Foreign Editor of *Le Monde* at the time of Suez (which he still is) has this to say about what he calls 'the Munich complex'.

ANDRÉ FONTAINE: If we try to make a list of all the reasons why Mollet and Pineau were tempted to do something against Egypt, I think we must put first a feeling of deception about Nasser himself. They very soon began to consider him as another Hitler. Many comparisons were made at that time between *The Philosophy of Revolution*, the main book of Nasser (which he actually did not write himself) and Hitler's *Mein Kampf*. I think it was something very silly because if you take the trouble of reading those books – really they have very little in common; and, of course, Egypt is by no means something which could be compared to Hitler's Germany. But that was the feeling at that time. I think the majority of the French people were much in agreement with that view. We all had at that time the Munich complex – just as Anthony Eden had – and when Nasser took the decision to nationalize the Suez Canal, this was taken as a major offence. If we had looked at that in cold blood I think we should have realized at that time that after all many countries in the world had taken such steps without prompting anyone to risk a war.

But between Egypt and France there were additional and more specific sources of hostility. To the French, Egypt was the country that was helping the rebels in Algeria. To the Egyptians, France was the country that was arming Israel.

On Algeria there was an attempt to come to terms. French opinion was split between traditional pro-Arabists, who were on the look-out for a revived role for France in the Middle

East; and the alternative policy of building up Israel against Egypt. We shall see in the next programme how the second party prevailed after assiduous and skilful lobbying by Israel in France. But the traditionalists were not easily defeated. They were strongest in the Foreign Ministry; and in March 1956 the Foreign Minister, Pineau, went to Cairo to see Nasser (as we have heard) and try to find out how far he was helping the Algerian rebels, and whether he could be made to stop. Here is Nasser's account:

NASSER: When Monsieur Pineau visited us he tried to reach a settlement about the Algerian question with me. But, I told him, I am not responsible for the Algerian revolution. He must know that the Algerians are responsible for that. I told him: 'Do not believe that the Algerian revolution is from outside: it is from inside.' There was no promise from me to Monsieur Pineau not to give any aid to the Algerians. I told him: 'It is our responsibility to help our Arab brothers everywhere.' He asked me about training, and about sending the Egyptians to the Algerians. I told him there are no Egyptians fighting with the Algerians. The Algerians are fighting alone. I told him we trained them. He asked me: 'Are you training them now?' There were no Algerians at that time in our country for training as soldiers.

CHILDERS: But you had already been sending arms, weapons, to the Algerians by then, had you not?

NASSER: Yes. Yes. From the first beginning to the end of the revolution.

Pineau's interview with Nasser gave the French only modified reassurance. And the effects were quickly wiped out because a few weeks later modern French fighter aircraft, promised to Israel the year before, actually arrived in Israel and provoked angry anti-French outbursts from Nasser – who was, of course, more closely concerned with Israel than with Algeria.

Nasser feared an attack by Israel, and he knew that Israel was being armed by the French. So one of the basic elements in his foreign policy in the years before Suez was a search for arms for Egypt. In 1955 he had entered into an arms agreement with Czechoslovakia. Childers asked him about his motives:

NASSER: First of all we were not able to get any arms from the West. We sent a delegation to London but the answer from London came back saying: 'Stop your opposition to the Baghdad Pact and we can talk about arms.' Then we got confirmed information that the committee[1] – which was from Britain, the United States and France – agreed to give Israel new weapons and new aeroplanes and the responsible country which had to deliver those weapons was France.

CHILDERS: So you knew about the major new French arms deal to Israel before the Czech arms deal?

NASSER: Yes.

It is never much good asking who starts an arms race. You have a situation in which two enemies are armed but not, in their own view, armed well enough for safety. So both go shopping for more arms. Each is alarmed by any move on the other side and uses that move to justify his own next move. For the record the principal episodes in the Egyptian-Israeli competition of the mid-fifties were these – in chronological order:

1954 A formal Franco-Israeli arms deal was concluded. Its existence was soon known in Cairo.

1955 Return of Ben-Gurion to the Government of Israel from his desert retreat, and heavy Israeli raid on Gaza in February. This was a reprisal for an Egyptian raid, but the Israelis inflicted five times as many casualties in return.

April: The signing of the Baghdad Pact.

September: Nasser's arms deal with Czechoslovakia.

---

[1] Presumably President Nasser is referring to the so-called Tripartite Declaration – *see programme III.* [Ed.]

November: A second Franco-Israeli arms deal, substituting ultra-modern *Mystère Fours* for *Mystère Twos.* (These were the aircraft which arrived in Israel in April 1956, just after Pineau's visit to Cairo.)

1956 Harold Macmillan visits Baghdad, and General Templer is sent to Jordan to try to get Jordan to join the Baghdad Pact. His mission fails. Dismissal of General Glubb by King Hussein in March.

By this time the Suez pattern is emerging. Part of it is clear for all to see: the anti-Egyptian Franco-Israeli *entente.* Britain is not yet associated with France or Israel; but because of the Baghdad Pact Britain too is regarded in Cairo as an enemy. And Anglo-French contacts are beginning.

The incident which ultimately brought Egypt's three enemies to take military action and brought them together was the nationalization of the Suez Canal Company. And the incident which occasioned the nationalization of the Company was the American decision not to help finance the Aswan Dam.

There has been a lot of debate about American motives on this point. I asked Robert Bowie of Harvard (see p. 7) about this. In 1956 he was an Assistant Secretary of State in Washington and one of a small group which helped Dulles to reach his decision.

ROBERT BOWIE: About the middle of July the Egyptians, who had been discussing financing the High Dam off and on with us and the World Bank, and with the British, indicated that they were going to send their ambassador back to Washington with the intention of accepting the proposal. This prompted Mr Dulles to hold an extensive discussion with his chief assistants and colleagues about the question of whether or not the United States should be prepared to go ahead with it. The reasons, which were pretty thoroughly canvassed at this two- or three-hour meeting in the middle of July, were principally these:

During the spring and early summer of 1956 it became

quite clear that the very large arms purchases which Egypt
had made from the Soviet Union had mortgaged a large part
of the resources which Egypt would otherwise have available
for devotion to the dam. The concern was that this might
mean that the foreign lenders or donors would end by
having put in their contributions and Egypt would not be
then in a position readily to put up its share. The fear was
that under these conditions the foreigners would be pushing
Egypt to fulfil its commitment and they would then be
subject to attack as interfering with the internal affairs of
Egypt. The Western powers might find themselves with a
half-fulfilled project. Not only would they not have gained
any political advantage from their assistance, but they would
even be in a defensive position. Meanwhile, the Soviets,
who would be able to put in other kinds of assistance, which
might be a good deal more showy since they might not take
fifteen years, would be able to capitalize on the discontent.

There were one or two other factors. The first was that the
states with riparian rights, the other states like the Sudan,
had not yet worked out how their interests were to be taken
care of in the construction of the Dam. Secondly there was
the problem of Congress, in the foreign aid discussions in
the Congressional Committees. In the spring and summer of
1956 the Congressional Committees had shown themselves
very reluctant to see any of the funds appropriated being
devoted to this Dam project. Indeed, the committees had
considered the insertion of specific provisions which would
seek to limit the use of funds for this purpose. Partly this
was due to the fact that the Dam was going to produce a
very substantial additional amount of cotton when it was
finally completed. It would only be used for irrigation of
land suitable for cotton – and a good many of the cotton
senators were not particularly eager to finance this additional surplus cotton. So that a number of these factors came
together. But I think the most important factor was the fear
that if you put up a very large amount of money, you might

end with not having a successful project – and also end with a situation which was negative in its political effects.

CALVOCORESSI: Was the recognition of Peking earlier that year a factor of any consequence?

BOWIE: I do not think it was really a factor with the administration. I think it may have been one additional prod to the Congress which was obviously disenchanted with Nasser.

CALVOCORESSI: Was the strong Egyptian reaction to this decision in July anticipated? Did you think that Nasser was going to react so strongly and take the sort of action that he did?

BOWIE: Certainly there was not the expectation that he would do what he did. Indeed, in the discussions, as I recall them, an enormous amount of effort was given to try to make the communiqué as unobjectionable as possible. I think anybody who is interested really ought to read the communiqué in the light of that fact. It says that this decision does not reflect on the friendly relations between the United States and the government and people of Egypt, the United States remains interested in the welfare of the Egyptian people, it is ready to consider any other kinds of assistance which might be worked out within the amounts which would be appropriated by Congress, and so on. In other words, I think there was a serious effort – and this was conscious – to try to see whether you could not at least take the rough edge off the decision which obviously was not going to be particularly palatable to the Egyptian Government.

But so far as President Nasser was concerned this effort does not seem to have been very successful. President Nasser has given this account of his own expectations about the Dam, and his reactions when the American decision was made public, in conversation with Childers:

CHILDERS: Did you expect that the Aswan Dam loans would be confirmed by Mr Dulles?

NASSER: No, I did not. I was sure that Mr Dulles would not help us by financing the Aswan Dam.

CHILDERS: What was your estimate of his reasons for not financing the High Dam?

NASSER: Because of the negotiations and talks, and so on. Then I met our ambassador before his return to Washington. He told me that if we accept some of the conditions which the World Bank and the United States want us to accept, they will give us the finance for the High Dam. I told him if we accept, they will not give us anything. And I was sure that the United States was not at all willing for the development of our country.

CHILDERS: Well then, when the news came from Washington on 19 July, that Mr Dulles had refused the loans, had cancelled them, you were not surprised at all by this?

NASSER: I was surprised by the insulting attitude with which the refusal was declared. Not by the refusal itself.

A few days after the announcement of the American decision President Nasser made a strong public attack on the Americans: and two days after that, in another speech on 26 July, he announced that the Suez Canal Company had been nationalized and its concession terminated.

The Suez Canal was and always had been Egyptian property. Nobody ever disputed that. But the Canal was affected by two agreements. By an international convention of 1888 Egypt was obliged to keep the Canal open at all times to all shipping. Egypt had been breaking the convention since 1948 by stopping ships carrying goods to or from Israel; but nobody except the Israelis had taken much notice. Secondly, by virtue of an even older agreement the running of the Canal was in the hands of a company with a resounding nineteenth-century name – the Universal Maritime Suez Canal Company. This Company had head offices in France and in Egypt. It was difficult to say whether, technically, it was a French company or an Egyptian company or a hybrid, but its capital, shareholders, directors and employees were almost entirely non-Egyptian. It had the right to run the Canal until 1968, when its concession would end.

Egyptians had been complaining about the Company years before Nasser came on the scene. They complained that the dividends paid to the shareholders were too large and that the sums spent on the Canal itself – for improving it and for the future generally – were too small. They complained that the Company was building up and hoarding enormous reserves outside Egypt, so that when the concession ended the Company would have extracted from Egypt a vast capital sum which it had never been intended to accumulate. Nasser had made plans in a general way to take the running of the Canal into Egyptian hands, but until 1956 he had no compelling reason for doing this before 1968, when he would get everything he wanted for nothing. To outsiders it seemed very possible that he would prefer to negotiate with the Company on the basis that the Company would disgorge some of its reserves, spend more on improvements, employ more Egyptians and possibly, in return, get its concession extended beyond 1968. But when the Aswan scheme fell through Nasser rounded on the Company and drove it out. He was – as I understand it – within his legal rights provided he paid the Company adequate compensation for the unexpired twelve years of the concession – which he said he would, though it was not clear where the money was to come from if the Canal dues were to be used to finance the Dam.

Erskine Childers asked President Nasser whether he had made plans to nationalize the company in the event of the Americans withdrawing from the Dam project:

NASSER: No. There were no plans for the nationalization but we studied the management by our mobilization department of the army in order to be ready to take over the Canal by the time of the end of the concession.

CHILDERS: Exactly when did you decide to nationalize the Suez Canal Company? The loan withdrawal came through on 19 July, and you nationalized on 26 July. What happened in between those days? When was the final decision taken?

NASSER: On 23 July because on the 20th Mr Nehru was here.

I was not able to have any meetings and discussions. The next day we began the meetings and discussions, and we studied the whole situation. On the 23rd we decided to nationalize the Suez Canal Company.

CHILDERS: When you nationalized the Company, were you surprised at the violence of the reaction in the West?

NASSER: I was surprised by the reaction of Britain. I was ready for the reaction from France, because the Company was a French company. But I was surprised by the reaction of Britain. I was waiting for reaction from Britain. I was surprised by the *amount* of the reaction of Britain.

CHILDERS: What did you think lay behind that? Can you remember what you thought the British intentions, or the British feelings, must be, when so strong a reaction came?

NASSER: Of course, we had studied the military situation of Britain, the economic situation of Britain – we had studied every aspect before the declaration of the nationalization. It was clear to us that Britain would not be ready to have any military movement before three or four months. We studied the deployment of the British troops and, of course, there were British troops in Libya, British troops in Germany. We thought at that time that it would be possible to reach a sort of a settlement during these three months.

This military and economic assessment by President Nasser and his advisers confirms the judgement of Monty Woodhouse (see p. 44). One might suspect hindsight; but another Englishman, who saw Nasser at that time, provides corroboration. Tom Little is a writer and journalist who has worked in the Middle East for twenty-five years. He was in Cairo throughout the Suez crisis. I asked him if Nasser was expecting to be attacked:

TOM LITTLE: Yes. I do not know at what time he began to be certain that it would happen, but I saw him – perhaps I was one of the last Englishmen to see him – in the middle of October 1956, and when I suggested that perhaps a compromise would be a good idea he said 'No, no compromise is possible. Sir Eden' – as he called him – 'Sir Eden intends to attack me and there is nothing I can do about it.' When I suggested to him that he could not hold out against Anglo-French forces, he said: 'But I do not intend to fight them. I intend to stand back and wait for world opinion to save me.'

We must remember that President Nasser's position in his own country at that time was nothing like as assured as it later became. He had scored some useful successes but he was still a comparatively new ruler. I asked Professor Vatikiotis, who is Chairman of the Centre for Near and Middle Eastern Studies in London University, how far the Egyptian Army and people were behind the President when the attack came:

P.J. VATIKIOTIS: In the spring of 1954 they had settled the issue of leadership and the power struggle in the Army – that had given President Nasser just over two years to consolidate his position within the Army. This brings us to summer 1956. Less than a year before that he had received new arms which means that not all these arms and training had been assimilated. At the beginning probably, pockets within the Army must have felt uneasiness at the suddenness of the attack, the magnitude of the attack of the Israelis – and the fact that the Egyptians after the first day of attack had to withdraw. It is also now quite certain that the first thought of the régime was making sure of the loyalty of the Army.

CALVOCORESSI: So that in your estimate for say a week or a few days at any rate after the Israeli attack on 29 October, Nasser had something to worry about, and the worry was chiefly directed at the Army because obviously the Army has power and the Army may contain pockets of discontent. What was it that removed this worry and removed this discontent?

VATIKIOTIS: Well, I would say three things. One of the things that strengthened Nasser vis-à-vis both the Army and the public was the fact that he did not lose his nerve. He kept quite calm and in complete control of the internal situation. In the second place I would say the way he dexterously responded to the international forces that were taking place at the time; and in the third place the fact that he appeared before the public as being attacked from all sides.

And here too is Mr Little on Egyptian attitudes:

LITTLE: The Egyptians were infuriated by the withdrawal of the loan offered by the United States, Britain and the World Bank for the building of the High Dam. They had great sympathy with Nasser. When he nationalized the Suez Canal Company, they were wildly delighted. Even the enemies of Nasser were with him at that time. Their delight was echoed all over the Arab world. It was natural. The Arabs, the Egyptians in particular, have always sought their dignity and independence and they felt that he had struck a magnificent blow for the liberty that they had claimed ever since last century. When the build-up of Anglo-French forces was started in Cyprus they were frankly astonished at first, but I do not think that they ever really believed that there was going to be a hot war over the Suez Canal. They did not show any great anxiety. They watched it rather cheerfully, as some by-play that was going on in the international political scene. Then suddenly there was the Israeli invasion. This took them completely by surprise. And twenty-four hours later there was the Anglo-French ultimatum. The anger of everyone seemed to me to be complete. People whom I knew to be sworn enemies of Nasser – rich people who had been impoverished by his policies – were suddenly strongly on his side and against the British.

CALVOCORESSI: Was there ever any chance of an alternative government to a Nasser government?

LITTLE: I have never thought so. I did not think so at the time. The whole affair happened at a time when Nasser was at his strongest. He had gained tremendously in prestige by the Czech arms deal in 1955. To the Egyptians and the Arab

world it seemed to them that Nasser had broken the mon-
opoly, the Western control of strategic positions in the Middle
East, and this they welcomed. From that moment he was
riding at the peak of his position. I do not think that it would
have been easy to find anyone to take his place. Presumably,
it was thought that perhaps Neguib could be resurrected
from his internment to take the leadership of Egypt again. I
doubt whether he would have done so; but even if anyone
could have been found to do so he could only have stayed in
office as long as the Anglo-French forces were in Egypt. To
keep anyone in office in Egypt would have meant the occupation of Egypt.

Another British observer on the spot was Robert Stephens
who was in the Middle East on a six months' special mission
for the *Observer* and got to Cairo twenty-four hours after
President Nasser's Alexandria speech. I asked him about
popular reaction in Cairo to the nationalization of the Canal
Company:

ROBERT STEPHENS: They were, of course, at first tremendously
excited that Nasser had taken this step; but also rather
apprehensive about what the reaction of the rest of the world
was going to be.

CALVOCORESSI: And this would be apprehension directed
chiefly against the British and the French, would it, rather
than the Israelis?

STEPHENS: No, I don't think anybody connected the Israelis
particularly with this situation or problem at that time. This
was a separate issue. Nasser's speech had connected the
nationalization with the cancellation of the aid for the Aswan
Dam and it was clearly intended to be a demonstration, and
was taken by the Egyptians to be, and the rest of the Arab
world to be, a demonstration of defiance and independence.
The Egyptians thought that they might be attacked either
by Israel for her purposes or by the Western powers, by
Britain and France. Chiefly, I think they feared the French

rather than the British; but I think that it never crossed their minds that this would happen together because it seemed to every Arab, certainly to the Egyptians, that this was so obviously politically disadvantageous to the West that it would be most unlikely.

President Nasser himself admits that at first he was worried about popular reactions to bombing and radio propaganda:

NASSER: Well, of course, I was worried about the reaction. On the day of the air-raids against us, I was worried and asking myself what would be the reaction of the people. There was blackout all over the country. Then I took my car and went to the Cabinet House. All the way I listened to the people raising the slogan 'We will fight, we will fight.' And this was fresh hope to me, because all my dependence by that time was on the people. Then on 2 November the air-raiders bombarded the transmission of our broadcast, and there was no broadcast. The only way for me was to go to El Azhar and give a speech. And I went to El Azhar in an open car and there were aeroplanes over Cairo attacking the military targets. But the people were in the roads by that time, and all of the time I was in the open car they were raising the slogan 'We will fight, we will fight.'

But fighting is not merely a question of spirit. It demands weapons. Egypt, as we know, had arranged to get Russian and Czech weapons. What kinds of weapons, and how much had arrived? On this part of the story I questioned John Erickson, the expert on Soviet military affairs, whom we heard in the last programme.

JOHN ERICKSON: The Russians and the Czechs between them had delivered to Egypt at least 80 Mig-15s – they were the kind of fighters used in the Korean war; and 115 Joseph Stalin, and T-34, heavy cruiser tanks – that, by the way, was the most modern type of equipment being used by the Soviet army itself and, of course, very much superior qualitatively to anything that the Israelis had. In addition the Russians had delivered several hundred self-propelled guns, armoured personnel equipment and supporting equipment. The crucial components were the 45 Ilyushin-28 strike bombers that the Russians had delivered to Egypt. So that is what you might call the hardware of Russian delivery to Egypt.

CALVOCORESSI: Now, given these various kinds of instruments of war, who was operating them?

ERICKSON: First of all let us take the bombers, the Ilyushin-28 bombers. These were clearly operated and were under the operations supervision of the Soviet and Czechoslovak personnel in Egypt. There were altogether three hundred and eighty Russian and Czechoslovak advisers. Now as for the pilots for these machines, a number of the pilots – altogether some two hundred air-crew, Egyptian by nationality – they were not in Egypt, they were being trained in Poland or in other training areas in the Communist *bloc*. Therefore, one has to argue that both the control and the handling of these machines was strictly a Soviet and a Czechoslovak affair – predominately, of course, a Soviet affair. The same would apply to the one hundred and fifty tanks.

I went on to ask Erickson what the Russians decided to do in this situation.

ERICKSON: Clearly what the Russians were concerned about was their strike bombers, these 45 Ilyushin-28s. I think they were not concerned, for example, that a few Soviet-built tanks should be seen in Port Said. But they were not prepared either to risk the operational employment or the capture of the Ilyushin bombers, for which reason these aircraft were flown either to Upper Egypt or flown out through Saudi Arabia into Syria. They withdrew all offensive capability from the Egyptians. Once you have withdrawn your strike bomber force then you have practically, to all intents and purposes, crippled the strike capacity of Egypt.

c

From the military point of view, therefore, Egypt was hamstrung in the face of the Israeli attack. It was also, as President Nasser realized, helpless against two powers of the order of Britain and France. But the military victory of the Israelis was followed by the Anglo-French fiasco with the result that the balance sheet of the Suez war has to be drawn up not in military terms but in political terms. It is with this balance sheet that we shall be concerned in the rest of this programme. How did the war affect President Nasser's position at home and in the Arab world, how did it affect the Arab-Israeli confrontation; how has it affected the positions of Britain and of France in the Middle East?

To both Professor Vatikiotis and Mr Little, President Nasser's fortunes look like a graph or curve which gets a boost from the Suez war, rises up to 1961 or 1962, then begins to fall back again. Here is Professor Vatikiotis:

VATIKIOTIS: It is clear that by the winter of 1956–57 Nasser had acquired a certain heroic image. It is also clear that he was convinced that the way international reaction to the Suez incident went there was an area to be exploited even further. By 1958 his position vis-à-vis the Arab world was very strong: the union with Syria; the undermining of his major rival Nuri Said in Iraq; the very touch-and-go situation in Jordan; the fairly successful opposition and practically nullification of the so-called Eisenhower doctrine in 1957 – so that between 1958 and 1960 or '61, one might say that Nasser's position as a proclaimed Arab leader was quite strong. With 1961, when he has to retrench at home, the so-called nationalization laws and the Socialist policy, which are now having their political effects in terms of a weakened position at home, did have an adverse reaction in many parts of the Arab world. For example, the break-up of the union with Syria; the retrenchment of other régimes at home which make it possible for them to integrate even their own enemies within their own establishment – I am thinking of places like

Jordan and so on; the fact that power in the Arab world for a while was going to the peripheries rather than to the centre – I am thinking of Saudi Arabia and then Kuwait playing at, let us say, the economic development broker. Nasser's Arab policy by 1962 was to a large extent a failure, if it was a policy to unite the Arabs under at least his leadership.

CALVOCORESSI: Partly because he wants to and partly because circumstances have made it go that way, since 1962 Nasser has concentrated on domestic affairs more than before.

VATIKIOTIS: With the exception, of course, of the Yemen.

CALVOCORESSI: And all this had an impact on his attitudes to Israel?

VATIKIOTIS: Yes, it had an impact – a definite one. His attitude was that it was not practical or feasible and was too risky to conduct any kind of military attack upon Israel, the so-called elimination of Israel, until all Arabs become revolutionaries, preferably on the Egyptian model.

CALVOCORESSI: When you said action against Israel was too risky, you had in mind, I believe, two things: one, a straight military risk that one had had clashes before, and they have always failed, and there is a limit to the number of failures that you can possibly afford in this particular field; and secondly, I think that you were indicating that he has been developing certain things at home and that these too would be put at risk, if he had a too adventurous foreign policy at the present time?

VATIKIOTIS: Very much so. Especially on the latter score, in the sense that there has been immense investment. There is a risk also in the sense that the new groups that have come up with this situation, whether they are in the army or whether they are just professionals – economists, planners, managers, what have you – are beginning in indirect ways, not necessarily direct democratic ways, to exert a certain amount of pressure.

Mr Little suggests that the basic element in President

Nasser's varying fortunes is how far he remains in tune with the varying climate of Egyptian and Arab intellectual opinion. I took up his earlier point of how Nasser gained by his arms deal of 1955 and by the failure of the Anglo-French attack in 1956, and I asked how long he remained at this peak of power:

LITTLE: It is difficult to fix a date, but I should put it roughly at about 1961. He was accepted, I think, up to that time, and perhaps for longer as the radical force in the area. He was, so to speak, the secular caliph looking after the Arab world. Although he had great economic difficulties, he did manage to survive and he got, of course, the finance for the High Dam which had been the cause of it all from Russia. But after 1961, particularly with the break of the union with Syria – which might be described as the high point – there seemed to me to be the beginning of the decline of his influence over the minds of the intelligent Arabs who are the effective political people in the whole Arab world.

CALVOCORESSI: Was that because he changed, or because they changed?

LITTLE: To some extent because he changed. I think he became more ideological in his approach to the problems than he had been before. After 1961 the Egyptians wanted a period of calm; they hoped that the lesson would have been learned, and Nasser would say: Right, now we will get down to looking after our own affairs. Instead he announced his Arab Socialist union and preached the Arab revolution. Then he went into the Yemen, a war which I am sure he thought he could win very quickly, but in which instead he got bogged down in a long blood-letting which could produce no permanent solution. Finally I think there was the recognition that in Egypt the socialization had not produced the economic benefits which had been expected of them – rising prices and shortages had deprived the working classes and the urban people, in particular, of the benefits they had derived from the revolutionary régime. The whole picture of the revolution in the Arab world was tarnished and there were a great many, perhaps the majority of, intelligent thinking Arabs now saying: For heaven's sake let us have a little peace, a little tranquillity in the area.

CALVOCORESSI: So as you see it this is a picture of a man who was a highly successful radical leader up to a point but now finds himself in a world which is beginning to have enough of revolution for the time being. How does this affect Arab-Israeli relations?

LITTLE: I think Arab-Israeli relations are affected by the conditions which have been produced in the area during this period. Clearly, if Nasser had been able to unite the entire Arab world behind him, the position of Israel could have been extremely precarious by now. It would have depended entirely, then, for its existence – physically as well as morally, so to speak – on the support of the great powers. Now with the disturbed condition of Iraq, with the Iraqi Army either at war in Kurdistan or keeping watch upon it, the Egyptian Army in Yemen, and the Syrian Army disturbed by its political, internal strife, I cannot see that Israel has much to fear. The strength of statements which are made against Israel now in the Arab world may appear to many people – and I think do appear to many Arabs – as perhaps a sign of weakness of *galam faadi*, of empty words.

These two experts both present the balance sheet of Suez very much in terms of President Nasser's personal achievements or failures, and this in itself casts light on the nature of the war's impact. Mr Stephens, while agreeing that one of the consequences of Suez was to strengthen Nasser, goes on to define these consequences in broader terms:

STEPHENS: Two immediate consequences were to confirm the position of Nasser as an Arab leader, to confirm the greater role of the two super-powers, Russia and America, in dealing with Middle East affairs as far as great power influence was concerned; and the third – again confirming rather than creating a new situation, but accelerating it – was the disengagement of Britain from the military position.

CALVOCORESSI: What about British policy? Britain has frequently been accused of dividing the Arabs for our own purposes. In the fifties it was the Hashemite Kings against Nasser and his friends. Today, some people say, it is King Feizal of Saudi Arabia in a similar role. Did Suez effect a basic change in Britain's attitude to the Arab world and Arab unity, or not?

STEPHENS: British policy had been based on two things: the use of military bases in order to deny the area to external powers, chiefly Russia in this case; and secondly the control of our oil interests there. The British disengagement really came to a head two years later in 1958, when you had the revolution which overthrew Nuri Said in Iraq and the end of the Baghdad Pact. And the fact that in spite of this the Americans who had intervened in the Lebanon and the British who had intervened in Jordan did not go on to try and reverse the revolution or to intervene in Syria, which was then linked with Egypt. The result of this crisis was to leave that area of the Middle East virtually a neutralized area from which the great powers kept out from the point of view of military intervention. So that the British then withdrew their actual military presence to a more peripheral area, but one very vital, which they considered very vital to them: the oil territory in the Gulf and down to Aden, which became the new headquarters.

Suez lingers on in British thinking about the Middle East, and even more so in Egyptian thinking about Britain. But according to André Fontaine things are quite different in Franco-Egyptian relations. I asked him about France's standing in the Middle East ten years after Suez:

FONTAINE: I think that all this affair has been completely forgotten. De Gaulle is very popular in the Middle East, not only in the Arab countries but in Israel too. I remember at the last presidential election in France, the first dispatches with approval of this re-election came both from Cairo and Tel Aviv which probably means that they do not have exactly the same view of what de Gaulle is really up to. But in Egypt, in Lebanon and Syria, everywhere I think in the Middle East, de Gaulle is a very, very popular figure. For two reasons: first of all he gave independence to Algeria, and this is an achievement which nobody in that part of the world is ready to forget; and the second reason is resisting the Americans. I think resisting the Americans is one of the main ambitions of all those countries, but they are too weak to do it; so since they contemplate a man who is strong enough to act in that direction, they admire him very much.

CALVOCORESSI: And we might add from a British point of view that France does not happen to be sitting in Aden, which makes it a great deal easier for you to repair your relations with Egypt.

FONTAINE: That is completely true.

Here to end the programme are President Nasser's own general conclusions on the impact of Suez:

NASSER: I was accused of many, many things. But all my object was, was to have complete independence in the Arab countries. Some people said Nasser wants to have an empire for himself. It is not a question of a person. As I said before, Nasser can continue for ten years. The Arab people in the Arab countries will continue for ever. So all that we do and all that we work for now is to have independent countries and united Arab countries; but united Arab countries do not mean an empire for somebody; it means to have a strong Arab nation.

CHILDERS: When you speak about the charge of wanting an empire it reminds me of the charge that Eden and Mollet made: that in your book in 1954 you had said that there was a role searching for a hero in the Arab world. Now what or who was the hero?

NASSER: The hero – that is to clarify, to appeal to people.

What is the role of the hero? It is not to dominate, but it is to ask and explain and remind the people about their past. Of course, when we were under foreign influence this was impossible; but after getting our independence, securing our independence, insisting about our independence – this was the real time for the role.

CHILDERS: Do you think that Suez could happen again?

NASSER: Yes, yes.

CHILDERS: Do you really think there could be another British or French attack on Egypt?

NASSER: You know, we insist about our independence, but we feel now that they do not like that. I want to add – the United States, they do not like what we say about our independence. They do not like what we feel about the Arab countries. They do not like our insistence to be completely independent. Of course there is also the supplies of arms to Israel. The United States gave Israel two hundred tanks through Germany; then two hundred tanks through the United States; then aeroplanes, helicopters, through Germany. So Israel now is full of arms, and still the policy of Israel is to force a settlement.

CHILDERS: You think that there might again still be an Israeli attack into Sinai?

NASSER: Yes, of course; because there is an Israeli threat continuously not only against Sinai – against Syria, against Jordan, against Lebanon.

CHILDERS: On the question of nuclear weapons today, would you be willing to sign a non-nuclear agreement in the Middle East? For example, to open your nuclear reactors to some kind of inspection by the United Nations if the Israelis agreed to this?

NASSER: Yes, we expressed this point of view and we said we accepted the safeguards of the United Nations. Israel refused to accept the safeguards of the United Nations. I want to say again that we are willing to accept any agreement about the limitation of using any atomic weapons in the Middle East and we agree about observation by the United Nations, not by any other country. We refuse to accept observation from the United States, as this means interference in our internal affairs; but with the United Nations we accept.

CHILDERS: Looking at one of the partners in Suez today, France – how would you estimate relations between the United Arab Republic and France today?

NASSER: We have good relations now with France.

CHILDERS: Although relations between Israel and France continue?

NASSER: But not as in the past, not as at the time of the Fourth Republic.

CHILDERS: What do you think British policy is towards the U.A.R. today, and in the Arab world? Has it changed since Suez?

NASSER: British policy continues to be hostile towards the United Arab Republic, towards us. Why, I do not know. They are under the impression that we are against them.

CHILDERS: But do you think that a British government would still, today, consider trying to overthrow your government by direct force, or indirect force?

NASSER: It is not a question of overthrowing my government. It is not easy and I think it is impossible. On the other hand, they support all our enemies. Whenever they see somebody who is hostile to us, or our enemy, they co-operate with them.

CHILDERS: Looking back then overall, what do you think was the outcome of Suez, the effect of Suez, first on Egypt?

NASSER: We were able after Suez to nationalize all the foreign assets in our country and by that Suez regained back the wealth of the Egyptian people to be used for the interests of the Egyptian people. Then, of course, on the other hand it was clear for the Egyptian people that they could defend their country and secure the independence of their country. So we mobilized ourselves for development and raising the standards of living of the people.

CHILDERS: Now, what do you think the effect of Suez was on the Arab nation, the Arab world as a whole?

NASSER: Well, of course, Suez helped the Arab nation, the Arab world, to regain confidence; and it proved to the Arab nation that Arabs are one nation because the reaction was not here in Egypt alone.

CHILDERS: Looking at international history throughout the world, if you were asked by an historian to say what the meaning of Suez was to world history in this mid-twentieth century, what would you say it was?

NASSER: Well, the meaning of Suez is that there is an end to the methods of the nineteenth century: that it was impossible to use the methods of the nineteenth century in the twentieth century. On the other hand, Suez gave confidence to many countries. I think Suez helped many of the African countries to be sure of themselves and insist about their independence.

3. Israel and the Middle East

A documentary by PETER CALVOCORESSI

First broadcast 14 July 1966

PETER CALVOCORESSI: In the last programme we looked at the Middle East through Arab, largely Egyptian, eyes. Tonight our viewpoint is Israel, and I feel I must begin by emphasizing a salient fact of Middle East geography. Israel is a very small country, about the size of Wales and only a dozen or so miles wide at one point. All its neighbours are enemies and, to take them at their own words, irreconcilable enemies, simply waiting for the right moment to extinguish the Israeli state for good and all. Israel must therefore be strong. It must at the very least be able to man its fences. More than that – at any rate this has been the dominant view – Israel must be able to sally forth into enemy country from time to time, to retaliate in at least equal measure against any raids on its own territory, and to keep its enemies impressed by its strength and its resolution.

This policy needs tools as well as guts. The tools are of course modern weapons, and getting modern weapons means having at least one powerful friend who is willing to supply them. Very soon after its establishment Israel decided that the only possible friend was France, and so with great skill and persistence the Israelis laid siege to key points in the French establishment at quite an early date.

I talked with two people who have gone into this Israeli lobbying of France in the course of writing books about the Suez war. The first, Michel Bar-Zohar, is an Israeli author whose book *Suez Ultra-Secret* has been a best seller in Israel. I asked him when the wooing of France by Israel started.

MICHEL BAR-ZOHAR: It started in fact about 1952–53. At that time there were some moves by Israeli diplomats and other special envoys to Paris who tried to get some weapons, some arms, from France. They succeeded on quite a modest scale. But the real success of the Franco-Israeli friendship, or alliance, was, I think, in 1954-55; and that was because at the time the Algerian war began and France was extremely anxious to have somebody who would fight against Nasser, against Egypt. I do not speak, of course, about the sympathy which French governments or the French people might have for Israel, but the fact that French people believed that Nasser, that Egypt, was the main supplier of arms and the main source of help for the Algerian rebels. This fact pushed France to help Israel more and more from the military point of view; in fact, to bring it about that Israel would be able to fight against Nasser and be some counter-balance, counter-weight, to Nasser in the Middle East. Since 1955 there was something in France which was called 'The Club' and which was composed of some Ministries which were in very close touch with anything which was connected with Algeria. There were also some generals, and some military people, in this Club, and they were sure that Egypt was the main force behind the rebels. They came to the Israelis and asked them to create special relations between themselves and this French Club, whose common enemy they pretended was Nasser. I may add to this: some members of this Club were members of the French Government, as a matter of fact.

CALVOCORESSI: You consider this was a contribution, an important contribution, to getting an arms agreement between Israel and France?

BAR-ZOHAR: Well, it became very, very important after the Government of Guy Mollet took power in France, because Guy Mollet and his party, the Socialists, were very close to the Israeli Socialists, the Israeli Labour Party. On the other hand, you had in the French government the Radicals who were very, very big partisans of French Algeria. So there was this coalition Government: on one hand you had the pro-Israeli Socialists; and on the other hand the anti-Egyptian, pro-French Algeria, people.

I should add that the traffic was not all one way. Israel had something France wanted as well as vice versa. As early as 1953 France made a secret agreement with Israel (revealed a year or so later) for the purchase of a patent in connection with nuclear development.

Another successful book on this subject is *Crisis: the inside story of the Suez conspiracy* by the Canadian writer, Terence Robertson. Mr Robertson too had found that the Franco-Israeli 'arrangements' went back well before 1956. I asked him how far:

TERENCE ROBERTSON: The earliest I was able to track it down to was about the summer of 1953, when Israel believed that the only other nation which had a fear of the Arabs that was identical to their own was France, because France had its problems in North Africa. And there was an identity of interests that the Israelis felt they might exploit. In my talks with Ben-Gurion he mentioned that by the time he sent Peres[1] to Paris in the autumn of 1955 he had already established a political co-operation with France over a long period before that, going back to 1953.

I also asked Mr Robertson whether he had got any confirmation from *Israeli* sources of what he had been told in France:

ROBERTSON: The Israelis have a deep regard for the French in as much as they feel that the French have not only helped them, but have carried through all the obligations they undertook. Therefore, the Israelis always told me 'Well what did you learn in Paris? We are not going to say anything unless you have been told it in Paris first.' This was the way of asking me what I knew. But in fact when I told them what I had seen – and I told them quite frankly – they did tend to confirm it. They would not go into details, but they would go into long explanations of the fact that they had to live under the gun, that they were surrounded by a ring of steel, and that they had to have an ally, they had to have a powerful

[1] Shimon Peres, Director-General of the Israeli Ministry of Defence.

ally, and they had to have one they could rely upon. And they had long before Suez found this ally in France, because of the identity of interests in view of the French involvement in Africa.

CALVOCORESSI: Neither party, neither the French nor the Israelis, are particularly concerned to make a secret of this, are they?

ROBERTSON: No, not in the slightest.

CALVOCORESSI: They do not feel they have anything to be ashamed of?

ROBERTSON: No. In fact, they are very proud of it. The French are very proud of the fact that they have honoured all their agreements – right through to the bitter end of the United Nations and elsewhere – to the Israelis; and the Israelis are eternally grateful to the French.

I myself went to Paris to find out how it was that Israel was so successful in getting French support. I talked to M. Christian Pineau, who was Foreign Minister in 1956, in his flat in Paris:

CHRISTIAN PINEAU: We decided to give support to Israel because it was for us a possibility to redress the situation in the Middle East. You understand what I mean?

CALVOCORESSI: Yes. When you were thinking of Nasser in these terms as a dangerous politician who was trying to extend his power outside his own country of Egypt, were you thinking primarily of the Middle East as we normally understand it or were you also thinking of the Algerian situation?

PINEAU: No. The situation of Algeria was quite different for us from the situation in the Middle East. But the nationalization of the Canal was for Nasser a great success, and among the Algerian people the success of Nasser was a success of the Arab people in general. For us it was very dangerous if we did nothing.

CALVOCORESSI: How far was there also at the same time in France and especially in left-wing circles in France a definite pro-Israeli feeling, either based on feeling for the Jewish people as a whole, or based on a feeling that these were the people who were conducting a real Socialist experiment in the Middle East?

PINEAU: Yes, it is true that in 1956 it was a Socialist Government – not all Socialist, but part Socialist Government – and the Socialist experience of Israel was very interesting for us. From a spiritual and political point of view the principles of the Government of Israel were for us much more sympathetic than the Nasser principles. But it is not the main reason. If Israel had not some particular reasons to engage in this Sinai campaign, I am sure the French Government would not decide to invade the Suez Canal.

CALVOCORESSI: Your main reason then is that you felt it to be necessary and expedient to build up in Israel a counterbalance to Nasser's power in Egypt. Now does this policy go back some years before 1956, and before the nationalization of the Canal Company?

PINEAU: Yes, maybe one, two years; the aid to Israel was for us a possibility of counter-balance, as you say, between Israel and Egypt. But it is since Nasser was in power in Egypt that we began to aid Israel with a big aid.

CALVOCORESSI: Big aid in terms of arms?

PINEAU: And supplies. Arms and supplies.

CALVOCORESSI: And up to 1956 then, the French policy was to help Israel with arms and supplies against what was regarded as an Egyptian menace, but at some point after 1956, after July 1956, am I right in thinking, the policy developed into something else which one might call a policy of co-belligerency. Is that right?

PINEAU: Yes. Maybe it is not so simple. (I speak personally: it is my point of view, maybe not the point of view of all the French members of Government.) For us, nationalization of Canal was very dangerous. First, because Nasser said we do not want the Israel Navy to pass through the Canal, and we thought at this period if Nasser does not want, it will be the same for the French Navy, for the English Navy. That is very dangerous for us because at this period we had and you had some very big interest in the Far East.

When he talks about navies M. Pineau is thinking particularly of *merchant* shipping. He then went on to make a second point which was new to me:

PINEAU: I was very interested by the aid to the underdeveloped countries and two months before the nationalization of the Canal I had deposed before the United Nations a project of aid to the underdeveloped countries. If we accepted the nationalization of the Canal it would be quite impossible to have a private and state capital for this aid. It is also true that if we had a discussion in the present time about aid to the underdeveloped countries everybody said it is quite impossible to do investments because of the possibility of nationalizations. It is much more important than people think.

One of the most skilled and constant observers of these matters is M. André Fontaine (see p. 36). I asked him what other motives France had for re-entering Middle Eastern politics:

ANDRÉ FONTAINE: First of all there was the feeling of solidarity with Israel. I think Israel had a lobbying action in Paris at that time which was very fruitful, very well conducted. Everybody in France was very happy with that. Then there was a feeling among the Radical components of the Government that a victory over Nasser would kill the roots of the rebellion in Algeria, and would bring about a possibility of finding a solution to that irritating problem. That was the reason why the Suez war was conducted and was at that time so popular in this country.

CALVOCORESSI: The reasons: first that Nasser was unreliable and dangerous; secondly that there was a need to settle the Algerian problem and that one way of doing it was to adopt this pro-Israeli policy in the Middle East; and third, this business of Socialist solidarity in Israel?

FONTAINE: Not only Socialist solidarity, although I should say it was the truth for Mollet himself. But for the public in France at large, a feeling of solidarity with Israel was explicit. Maybe we had more or less a feeling of responsibility for what happened to the Jews during the war, you know, and we felt that something was due to them.

The Israeli approach to France, and the French response, had to be secret because what Israel wanted was weapons, and France was not strictly speaking free to supply these weapons. In 1950 – after the end of the fighting between Israel and its Arab assailants – the United States, Britain and France had agreed to keep the supply of arms to the Middle East low and balanced. The object of this so-called Tripartite Declaration was to prevent an arms race between Arabs and Israelis. Israel's policy was to induce France to arm Israel in contravention of the Tripartite Declaration.

Broadly speaking there are two phases in the Franco-Israel alliance. In the first and longest, what the Israelis wanted was French arms. This phase began, as we have heard, some years before the war of 1956. Supplies were stepped up in the last twelve months after changes of Government in both Israel and France, and especially after Egypt's Czech arms deal. When Egypt began to get Russian arms, Israel assumed that Egypt would reply to any Israeli offensive by bombing Tel Aviv and other places in Israel. To meet this threat Israel not only needed supplies of French material; it was also essential for Israel to have active French support in the shape of air cover—and, as we shall see later, British help in the air too. In the second phase, which begins with the expropriation of the Suez Canal Company, Israel was able to get this support.

When the fighting began, the balance of forces in the air, as seen by the Israeli Commander-in-Chief, General Dayan, looked like this. Here is an extract from his recently published diaries:[1]

[1] *Diary of the Sinai Campaign* by Major-General Moshe Dayan, Weidenfeld & Nicolson (1966).

DAYAN DIARY: The Egyptian Air Force is composed exclusively of jets, whereas ours is still based on quite a few piston-engined aircraft. As far as we know the Egyptians have received from the Russians about 200 Mig-15 fighters and some fifty Ilyushin-28 bombers. . . .

We have so far identified eight squadrons of jet fighters. . . . Against these eight jet squadrons, we can put into action in Sinai five jet-fighter squadrons. . . . As for bombers, we have two piston-engined B-17 planes against two Egyptian squadrons – thirty to sixty planes – of Ilyushin-28s.

I know that in all the European armies piston-engined aircraft have been assigned to the scrap-yards; but we shall use ours. We have sixty-four of them—twenty-eight Mustangs, thirteen Mosquitos, twenty-one Harvards, and the two B-17s. Altogether, then, counting 'the rabbits and camels' together, we have at our disposal 143 planes – roughly half jet fighters and half piston-engined aircraft – as against the 150 to 250 Egyptian planes, all jets.

The commander of our Air Force argues that even these comparative figures are optimistic and do not reflect the true picture. According to him, of our thirty-seven Mystères, only fourteen are serviceable, and even they are armed only with 30-mm. cannon, as we have not yet received the rockets and bombs for them. Moreover, most of our pilots are still novices, have not yet been in action and have not even managed to complete their full training. Our best planes, the Mystères, we started getting in April of this year, and most of them arrived only in August [1956] – just two months ago.[1]

These Mystère fighters are Mystère-4s, the most modern jet fighters made in Europe at that time. After the Czech arms deal Israel had got the French to supply Mystère-4s in place of Mystère-2s promised under an earlier 'agreement'.

Mr Ben-Gurion himself has recorded, at the Sdeh Boker

[1] pp. 80–1.

Kibbutz in the desert roughly halfway between Tel Aviv and Eilat, his account of how Israel sought for arms and allies.

DAVID BEN-GURION: We made attempts to get arms from America, which was a complete failure. But we succeeded in getting arms from France to a very large extent. For a long time it was a secret. They came not to a port, but somewhere on the sea at night in coloured ships that you could not see from above. We were waiting for them and immediately we took the arms down into the centre, to our Army. This went on perhaps for about six or eight weeks. In order to keep it secret I called together all the editors of our papers and I told them not to publish anything and none of them did publish anything. When it was finished, with the agreement of France I told Parliament. One of our poets wanted to see one night how it was done, and he was very much impressed, and he wrote a poem about it. I would not allow the poem to be published. On the afternoon I told Parliament about it for the first time, the poem was published in our Hansard. I published it there. With the arms we got from France we believed that we could stand against Egypt.

The crucial event in the development of the Franco-Israeli partnership against Egypt was the expropriation of the Canal Company. More than that, the expropriation not only transformed the Franco-Israeli association but also created a tighter Franco-British association, and so led eventually to the Franco-British-Israel partnership. Both Mr Bar-Zohar from the Israeli side and Mr Fontaine from the French agree that the expropriation was a catalyst.

BAR-ZOHAR: France was very, very interested in crushing Nasser in one way or another. France helped Israel from the military point of view, as you have mentioned, expecting that Israel would not otherwise be able either to defend itself, or to break Nasser in case there was war. France was interested – and that is very important to mention – to go into a war against Nasser, even before the Suez Canal was nationalized by Egypt. But these people, these Ministers in France – there were some Ministers who were interested in this kind of thing – could not think of any pretext, any excuse, for France going to war against Egypt. But when in the middle of 1956 the Suez Canal was nationalized, France decided to go to war against Egypt because she had found the excuse – I think, the ideal pretext for making this war. She wanted to do so before, but could not.

I asked André Fontaine when France moved from being an arms supplier to becoming a co-belligerent:

FONTAINE: I think just after expropriation. The first step towards Israel was to ensure that the arms deliveries would be assured faster even than before. There was no idea at that time of military co-operation. The idea was to make something with Britain, but, as you know, Britain was more or less under American influence. On two occasions, due to the reaction of Washington, the military operations which had more or less been decided against Egypt were postponed. So at the end of September 1956, the French Government was approached by the Israeli Government which had the idea of a common Franco-Israeli action against Egypt. I think Ben-Gurion had been for long a defender of the idea of preventive war; and if you read Moshe Dayan's memoirs[1] he puts it in very clear terms. But what Israel needed at that time was an air cover to attack Egypt since the Soviet had provided Egypt with a very important number of aircraft of various types. So Israel approached France. But, on our side, we lacked some types of aircraft, especially middle-range bombers. I think it was under French influence that finally Britain accepted a role in that action – the Canberras of the R.A.F. intervened in the battle against Egypt from the first day of the Israeli intervention, a fact which had been denied several times but which now can be discussed. So

[1] op. cit.

finally France acted as an intermediary power between Israel and Great Britain.

We have now got a picture of the Franco-Israeli partnership in political and military terms. Before we go into the actual war we need to ask one more question about the temper of Israel. By 1955 or thereabouts Israel was not only arming, but was coming to the conclusion that the arms would have to be used. I spoke to Jon Kimche who was then the editor of the *Jewish Observer and Middle East Review* and who has written about the Middle East and travelled in it for the past twenty years. I asked Mr Kimche why Israel felt that way by 1955:

JON KIMCHE: There were two or three main reasons. In the first place, there was the aftermath of the arms deal of the Egyptians with the Russians, which introduced a considerable amount of new equipment on the other side of the fence, so to speak; and the Israelis saw it gradually assembling at their end of the Sinai desert. There was quite a strong concentration of Egyptian forces in that area by midsummer of 1956. That was one reason. It puzzled them. They were not certain about the Egyptians, but it worried them. Then something about which the Israelis were quite clear was the continuing and mounting border raids from the Gaza strip into the border settlements. These continued almost nightly. They varied from thieving, stealing of water pipes, chickens, to generally worrying the settlers. Some were killed, some were wounded. But the general feeling of unrest was very noticeable, when I was there in that summer. A number of the settlements began to report the departure of settlers back into the towns. The whole settlement programme, in a sense, was being jeopardized by this; and in another sense there was the security of the state, because the army people and the police began to worry as to where this infiltration could lead. How far could the infiltrators go? Could they perpetrate terrorist acts say in the towns, in a Tel Aviv cinema, or on the roads against passing traffic? So that generally there was a feeling of disquiet and unrest and there seemed to be nothing that one could do to stop the actual raids except by a massive retaliation action.

CALVOCORESSI: Then only in 1955 Mr Ben-Gurion returned to office. What was the significance of that?

KIMCHE: Originally the main reason for that was purely internal. There was an attempt to tighten up the discipline in the higher ranks of the Army by putting in a Defence Minister whose word was law and who controlled the military rather than the other way round. But Ben-Gurion's very presence at the head again began to concentrate attention on the security problem of the state.

Israel's attack on Egypt was, as we know, launched on 29 October. What were the objectives? The two most important aims were to ease the blockade of Israel by opening the Gulf of Aqaba to Israeli commerce, and to put a stop to Egypt raids across the borders, which had become very heavy and frequent.

The Gulf of Aqaba runs up from the Red Sea, through the Straits of Tiran. It is bounded by Egyptian and Saudi Arabian territory but at the north end of it is the Israeli port of Eilat and seven miles of Israeli coastline. By closing the Straits of Tiran the Egyptians were able to strangle Eilat and prevent Israel from trading by sea with countries to the south and east. The closing of the straits supplemented Egypt's refusal to allow ships or goods for Israel to go through the Suez Canal. It was vital for Israel to remove this grasp on its windpipe, and it did so. Eilat, which had fewer than 1,000 inhabitants in 1956, now has over 13,000.

The second immediate objective of the Sinai campaign was to stop the border raids. Before this Israel had adopted a tit-for-tat policy. Every Arab raid was followed by an equivalent Israeli riposte. But some time during 1955 or 1956, with the raids getting heavier and more frequent, Ben-Gurion decided that this was not enough.

On the Egyptian front one way – perhaps the *only* way – to stop this murderous nuisance was to strike an exemplary blow at the Egyptians in the Sinai Peninsula.

The Israelis did not, as far as the evidence goes, indulge in any mad dreams about taking Cairo or even the Suez Canal. The plan was to get control of the whole of the Sinai Peninsula in seven to ten days; the heights to the east of the Canal were their furthest objective. Israeli forces would then sweep down southwards to lift the Egyptian blockade of the Straits of Tiran, and finally they would mop up the Gaza strip on Israeli's south-west frontier.

Here is Mr Ben-Gurion's own account of how these aims were first achieved and then partially frustrated in the one-week war.

BEN-GURION: On 28 October there was a meeting. It was Sunday. We held all the meetings on Sunday morning. It was a meeting of our Government. I gave them the reasons why we had to attack on one side the Gaza strip, on the other side the centres of the Fedayen. I told them that we must destroy the bases of the Fedayen in Sinai. And this was our aim in invading Sinai, although we did not regard Sinai as part of Egypt. Not a single Egyptian lives in Sinai – only a number of Bedouin here and there. But – I told the Government – 'You will not be able to stay there because Russia and America will not let us and we cannot do anything against these two great powers. So you should not have any illusions that we are going to conquer the Sinai desert.'

This was on the morning of 28 October. We began entering Sinai the night of 29 October, the following day. In a few days we really got the whole of Sinai in our hands. The furthest place which we occupied was Sharm-e-Sheikh which is near the Straits of Aqaba. And this was our main aim.

We received an ultimatum from France and England that we must retire ten miles from the Suez Canal. The same ultimatum was sent to Egypt. We agreed. We did so because from the beginning we had no intention of going into Egypt. And I told this to the Government: we have only to deal with the bases of the Fedayen in Sinai; and we would stay as long as necessary to ensure that these attacks by the Fedayen should stop. We received from the Security Council an order to stop. We replied: all right we will stop – because we were actually finished before that. No Egyptian was left inside Sinai. I think that the French and the English, especially the English, were not very happy about our acceptance of this order. They used their veto in the Security Council. Then the Assembly of the United Nations was called together. The Assembly ordered us to withdraw. We refused. We said: until we have guarantees that these attacks will not be repeated, we cannot withdraw. Secondly, until we have assurance that the freedom of navigation at least in the Aqaba Straits will be free we must stay in Sharm-e-Sheikh. Then they told us that they were not sure that they could get a majority of two-thirds in the Assembly of the United Nations, that we have the right to defend ourselves by force if we are prevented from free navigation in the Aqaba Straits. The American declaration made by Cabot Lodge was not satisfactory. Then I received a letter from Eisenhower himself saying that: 'You will have no reason to regret', and that it would be all right. I knew Eisenhower before he became President. I know you can rely on his word. When I received his letter, I called the General Staff together and I explained to them the reasons why I recommended to the Government that we withdraw. When I finished, I asked one of them – who I knew had the courage to answer me even if he did not agree with me – 'Are you convinced now?' He said, 'No, I am not convinced.' I asked him: 'Do you withdraw?' He said 'Of course. . . .'

Since then we have had less trouble with the Gaza strip. I do not say there was no trouble at all, but much less than we had before. So the main aims which we had in going into Sinai were achieved.

And here, from his diaries, are General Dayan's own statements on how far Israel's aims were achieved:

DAYAN DIARY: Three major purposes were achieved: freedom of shipping for Israeli vessels in the Gulf of Aqaba; an end to the Feydayen terrorism; and a neutralization of the threat of attack on Israel by the joint Egypt-Syria-Jordan military command. . . .

The military victory in Sinai brought Israel not only direct gains – freedom of navigation, cessation of terrorism – but, more important, a heightened prestige among friends and enemies alike. . . . And the sale of arms for her forces ceased to be conditional upon prior agreement among the 'Big Powers' – the United States, Britain and France.

The main change in the situation achieved by Israel, however, was manifested among her Arab neighbours. Israel's readiness to take to the sword to secure her rights at sea and her safety on land, and the capacity of her army to defeat the Egyptian forces, deterred the Arab rulers in the years that followed from renewing their acts of hostility. The Sinai Campaign was not intended as a preventive war. It was not meant to forestall a sickness but to cure a situation already sick – to breach an existing blockade of Israel's southern waters, and to put an end to rampant terrorism and sabotage. But in fact it did have the effect of checking Arab ambitions to do harm to Israel. It is not by chance that the President of Egypt, Gamal Abdul Nasser, bids the Arab States to refrain from attacking Israel as long as they have not strengthened their forces. He makes this plea not because he has stopped seeking Israel's destruction but because he has learned to respect the power of her army.[1]

In fact it seems that the Egyptians *were* taken by surprise because Israel had given the impression that it was about to move against Jordan; and the Egyptian Air Force *was* kept out of the battle by Anglo-French action:

[1] pp. 203–7.

DAYAN DIARY: *31 October:* the Egyptian Army itself was taken completely by surprise. Despite the news published several days now in the world Press about our mobilization of reservists and our war preparations, the Egyptians never guessed that these moves were directed against them. Their Chief of Staff, Abd-el-Hakim Amer, left five days ago with a group of his senior officers on a visit to the Jordanian and Syrian armies, and he returned to Egypt only yesterday, as planned. I cannot imagine that he would not have hastened back sooner if he had suspected that something was likely to happen any day on his borders.[1]

1 November: The Anglo-French bombing of Egyptian airfields which started last night has neutralized the capacity of the Egyptian Air Force to operate against us. Even before this, throughout the first night of the campaign (29 October) and the two days of fighting which preceded the Anglo-French action (30 and 31 October), Egyptian air activity did not extend beyond the boundaries of Sinai. The neighbouring Arab States, Syria and Jordan, who were asked to attack Israel from the air and who promised to do so, in fact did nothing. Actually, the Egyptian Air Force did send over Ilyushin-28 bombers on two occasions, on the nights of the 30th and 31st, one bomber on each mission, but they dropped their bombs on open ground, far from city or village, without discrimination and without causing damage.[2]

Israel's campaign was a complete military success. Did it also achieve its long-term purposes? Mr Abba Eban, now Israel's Foreign Minister, assesses the gains ten years later. He is speaking at his home in Rehovoth:

ABBA EBAN: Our gains have been very substantial. In the first place there is now peace on our southern frontier. Gaza used to be a source of constant eruption into Israel, destruction of life, insecurity to property. Now, since the Sinai campaign and the establishment of the international arrange-

[1] pp. 90–1.   [2] pp. 108–9.

ment in Gaza, we have had peace on our southern frontier. Even more important has been the opening of the Straits of Tiran and the Gulf of Eilat to normal traffic. Across the Gulf of Eilat we have established a network of relations with the countries of Africa and Asia. These are the two most tangible and substantial gains. But in addition there has been a psychological gain. Israel no longer has a sense of brooding fear concerning her survival. I see no reason to believe that we shall not be able in the coming years also to maintain a balance of strength which is not one of equality in quantity, but which is sufficient to dissuade our neighbours from attack.

Mr Eban confirmed that there is still no traffic to or from Israel through the Suez Canal. But, he went on:

EBAN: The practical significance of this for us has been greatly reduced. Since we opened our traffic by sea through the Gulf of Eilat, we are now able to export and import to and from the countries of East Africa and of Asia by another channel. In other words we have rights to use the Suez highway, but there is now a parallel highway which leads to the same place.

So much is made nowadays about the significance of Eilat that I found myself wondering if Israel was being completely reoriented by the opening of this back door looking more to Asia and Africa than to the west. And I also wanted to find out how far Israel, which is after all so well fitted to be the animator of the Middle East's economy and culture, feels excluded from playing a part there. I talked about these points to Mr Elie Kedourie, Professor of Politics at the London School of Economics and Editor of *Middle Eastern Studies*.

ELIE KEDOURIE: My impression is that Israel, although it wants for political and economic reasons to establish as cordial and close relations as possible with Asian and African states, is really a European kind of place. The ideals, the achievements, the needs are those of a European economy, and the politics are very much a European kind of politics. In the things that matter – namely social and cultural attitudes – Israel is not, it seems to me now or in the very near future, going to be very much affected by this development. It is very difficult of course to say that Israel is exclusively European or exclusively Middle Eastern. Obviously, it is a bit of both. So far as politics go, so far as interchange across international boundaries go, Israel is certainly cut off and on the level of political argument the Israelis can say that this is regrettable – that they could do much to help their neighbours if only their neighbours would let them. But, it seems to me, again on the level of culture and society, there is very little difference between Israel and her immediate neighbours in their aspirations for a European kind of economy. The Arabs just as much as the Israelis want to be a kind of Sweden or a kind of California.

I am sure that Professor Kedourie is right in saying Arabs and Israelis both want to live in a sort of Sweden or California. But if they are to do so, they must do so together. So there remains the question of Arab-Israeli relations. How have they changed in the ten years since the Sinai campaign? Mr Eban is optimistic:

EBAN: I have to distinguish here between the official view, the dogma of the establishment as it were, and the real view. Now the official view is not changed. The central dogma of Arab nationalism is that Israel will one day disappear in a great wave of violence. There is this apocalyptic vision of a war which is going to change the map of the Middle East and restore this country to its previous character, to its pre-Israeli character. That is the dogma. The question is how far that is believed. President Nasser clings to the doctrine itself, but he always finds reason for postponing its realization. He keeps saying: one day we are going to wipe Israel off the map, but not now, not this week, not this month, not this year – other things are more important and more urgent. Well, postponement of a dream is very similar in effect to the relinquishment of it. There are other Arab countries which are much more concerned to prevent being dominated by Nasser than to engage Israel. So I would sum up by saying that on the plane of rhetoric, of education, of indoctrination, the aggressive dream still exists. But it is becoming increasingly pushed into the realm of rhetoric, and in point of fact very little is being done by the Arab States to bring this doctrine into fulfilment.

Professor Kedourie is not so sure that, in the Middle East, rhetoric belongs to the world of fantasy and not to the real world. I asked him whether he thought it was right to treat the noises of hostile propaganda as though they did not matter very much in the field of action. In his answer he used the Palestine war of 1948 as an example of how rhetoric can affect action:

KEDOURIE: It is said that as a practical issue in international politics the Palestine question has now receded, there is no danger of war-like activities, that in fact 1948 is not likely to be repeated. If this argument is based on the assumption that now it is only a question of rhetoric, a question of propaganda, and that the situation was otherwise in 1948, then the assumption is mistaken. The more one looks at the war of 1948, the more one sees that it also was a product of rhetoric, the more one can see that a rational computation of advantages and disadvantages accruing to the different parties in this dispute would not have necessarily resulted in the conclusion that a war was from the point of view of the Arab states the best thing that could happen. In fact I tend to think now that 1948 was an unnecessary war. But it happened, whether necessary or not, and it happened, it seems to me more and more, because of that realm of rhetoric which Arab politics naturally inhabits, inhabited then and inhabits now.

I would not myself want to dissent from an authority like Professor Kedourie and I cannot help having an uncomfortable feeling that he is right. But it is possible to be more optimistic, to feel that the facts of the last ten years have already begun to change the atmosphere. Michel Bar-Zohar, from the point of view of one of Israel's new citizens, sees it this way:

BAR-ZOHAR: Israel has succeeded in creating a situation in the Middle East where a peace, a factual peace does exist. You see, there is no treaty, but from the Egyptian side there have been no attacks and no provocation against Israel in this interval. I want to add something here. I think – and this I cannot tell you for sure because I have not seen any documents about it – but I think that some very important Israeli leaders hoped that this attack of Israel on Sinai, and later the decision of the United Nations to put the United Nations Emergency Force on the Straits, on the Sinai Straits, might lead to the fall of Nasser himself. I cannot give you any document on it, but I have the impression that they just played with this idea. Well this was a deception because Nasser is as strong as he was there then, and I think even stronger today.

CALVOCORESSI: And when you speak of Israel having secured peace in the Middle East this is to me a slightly curious idea. There seems to be a prolongation of an armistice, a prolongation of a truce. But it is surely an uneasy state of affairs. Or do you think that fundamentally the position is now very much easier, and that the next years are going to be even easier still?

BAR-ZOHAR: Yes, I think so, and I shall tell you why. When I said peace in the Middle East I spoke specially about the relationship between Israel and Egypt. Of course this is not a peace, there is not a peace treaty, and the two countries are formally in a state of war. But on the other hand from the factual point of view, as a matter of fact, there are no fights, no incidents between Israelis and Egyptians. If you take it in the context of the problem of the Israeli Arab dispute, and if you see all these words and these feelings which are

very, very full of hatred on the Egyptian side against Israel,
I think that the fact that there are no incidents on the frontier
is already a very big success, and can bring with the years
to come the creation of a new atmosphere which could very
strongly help to bring peace to this part of the world, even
if peace takes so many more long years to come.

If you are an optimist – and how can you live in Israel if
you are not! – you have to take a fairly long view. From their
different points of view Mr Eban and Mr Kimche both do.
Israel's Foreign Minister reiterates the persistent Israeli faith
in keeping strong:

EBAN: The fact is that we have just as strong a balance of dis-
suasive strength now as before, perhaps even greater since
our sources of supply are more variegated. The United States
has recently played an active role in increasing Israel's defensive strength in the anti-aircraft domain and in armour and
in air power; our traditional sources in France and Britain
and elsewhere still remain open in accordance with discussions that we have with their governments. We are maintaining the balance of strength within the conventional formula;
and I am certain that our real problem arises from the build-
up of conventional strength by our neighbours. We found
methods of answering this challenge by increasing our own
strength and I think that that position will continue to pre-
vail. Moreover, it is a tenet of our policy not to be the first
to initiate a new stage in the arms escalation. We were not
the first to produce jet fighters, jet bombers, submarines,
heavy tanks, and now missile-carrying torpedo boats. In each
case Egypt, through its connections with the Soviet Union,
pushed the arms race up another notch and we responded –
this policy continues to dominate our thinking. We are not
going to be the first in any quantitative development of the
arms race and therefore whatever we do is always a reaction
to the efforts of our neighbours in that direction. Therefore,
if I were an Arab contemplating the reality, I should be very

sceptical indeed. Apart from the balance of strength, international influences are all working the other way, they are
working towards a consecration of the *status quo*, a crystalli-
zation of the existing territorial and political structures. That
is a trend throughout the world. I even include the Soviet
Union amongst those powers whose general policy is oriented
towards the preservation of existing territorial and political
facts, and not to revolutionary destruction of existing territorial and political structures. Therefore, both politically
and militarily, the dream of Israel's elimination becomes less
and less rational and I believe that there are rational elements
in the Arab world capable of making this analysis and capable
of drawing conclusions from it. Even if they want us to
disappear, I do not believe they think that we are going to.

Mr Kimche stresses, too, not only the changes that have
taken place along the borders but also the striking changes
in Israel's foreign relations:

KIMCHE: One has to experience the period before Suez, and
the period after, to realize what a difference it made. I mean,
in ten years there has been virtually no serious border incident in the south. Not only has there been no border incident, but the whole attitude – not only of Israel, but also of
the other countries in the area – has changed. For example,
Jordan has been much more peaceful.

It also introduced something else. Because of this freezing
of the Israel-Egyptian confrontation, it put the strain elsewhere. One result of this ten years' relative quiet was that it
enabled the Arabs to begin to sort out their differences
among themselves. For some reason or other, once the Israelis
had exploded in 1956 the Arabs felt that they would not
explode again quite so soon. It was possible for the Arabs
to have their differences without having to worry about
Israelis exploiting them. And this, of course, has happened.
This has changed the whole situation in the Middle East.
Today therefore the situation is not that Israel is confronted

by an United Arab world, but that there is a divided Arab world.

CALVOCORESSI: What about the great powers?

KIMCHE: True, there has been a tremendous change. Israel was a kind of tolerated friend in 1956. The British were uneasy to go along with her. The French were quite open about their 'alliance'. Elsewhere Israel had very few friends and a great many enemies and opponents. Since then Israel is on the best of terms with Britain, with France, with Germany, with a great many of the African countries with whom she has very close relations, so that she is no longer an isolated country, even among the new nations in the world.

CALVOCORESSI: What about the Americans and the Russians?

KIMCHE: Well, one of the big and probably the biggest unanswered questions of Suez which arose only after the event was: what was the purpose of a great deal of the material that was found in Sinai at the time? And whether there had been, whether Khruschev at that time had thoughts of having a kind of Cuba in the Mediterranean. At that time it did not come off. But since then the Russians had begun to establish themselves much more effectively in the Middle East. They have got a very sound base in Egypt. They are now developing one in Syria. They have a very sound one in the Yemen.

CALVOCORESSI: When you say they have a sound base, are you talking about military material?

KIMCHE: No. They have what the Americans used to call real estate. In other words they have got an ally who uses the same equipment as they do, where they have stocks of equipment, a possibility of using it if they wanted to. But I do not think this is really the main point. They have an ideological ally now which is much more important in the new context of this contest for the influence in the Middle East.

CALVOCORESSI: Ideology? You are not talking about communism?

KIMCHE: Near-communism! If you look now at the situation in Egypt and the last speeches of President Nasser, the

D

speeches in Syria, the general organization, the new economic policy – it comes very close to it now.

CALVOCORESSI: I would like to press you on this. It is a very
interesting point. If this is near to communism, ideolog-
ically speaking, does this also mean in your view that these
countries are abandoning the non-alignment which was a
prominent feature of their attitudes in external affairs in the
fifties?

KIMCHE: I think today there is hardly any pretence any longer
of non-alignment in either Egypt or Syria or the Yemen.
The real test is still in countries like Iraq, Algeria, and one or
two others.

However much the Arabs may be divided today, Israel can
never be sure that some powerful combination may not be
formed against it tomorrow. So the competition in arms goes
on. And since 1956 it has acquired a nuclear overtone. At
present Israel is generally credited with being three to five
years ahead of Egypt – the only Arab state remotely in the race.
But Israel's technological lead is to some extent offset by its
extreme vulnerability – due to its smallness. President Nasser
has said that he would accept U.N. inspection of nuclear estab-
lishments. Israel has so far refused – mainly on the plea that it
is unfair to introduce inspection for *nuclear* weapons only, ex-
cluding inspection of conventional weapons which are what its
enemies actually possess. But for the time being the real arms
race in the Middle East is still in the conventional field –
where it was, in fact, ten years ago.

4. Some Evidence of Collusion

A documentary by PETER CALVOCORESSI

First broadcast 18 July 1966

PETER CALVOCORESSI: We come in this programme to the issue called collusion. Because charges of collusion have stirred deep emotions it is exceptionally important to try to define what we are talking about. Collusion means co-operation; but not just co-operation. It means co-operation of a shady, disreputable or fraudulent kind. It also means, in this context, co-operation between Britain and Israel; and not between anybody else.

Now a charge of collusion is not a charge relating to the content of a policy pursued. A charge of collusion relates to methods, not to content. The allegation is that a policy, which may be a good policy or an unworthy one, is so conducted that leading statesmen do things that they ought not to do. What is it that they do that they ought not to do? Answer: deceive. According to the Oxford Dictionary collusion requires deceit, and an intention to deceive.

I want to stress the point that statesmen often do things secretly and have to do them secretly. Secrecy by itself is no crime in international relations any more than it is in private ones. If the British Government had negotiated a secret treaty with Israel it could not, on these grounds alone, be accused of doing anything wrong or unusual. The wrong-doing comes not from the act itself but from denying or obscuring it.

The charge in this case is that British Ministers entered into discussions with Israel and into a formal agreement; *and*, either explicitly or by implication, denied that they had done so. And – one final qualification – let me make it quite clear that in this programme I am not out to argue whether Britain should or should not have collaborated with Israel. I am concerned to elucidate whether it did and how far and how.

On 31 October – two days, that is, after the Israeli attack, and before the Anglo-French landings – Mr Gaitskell referred in the House of Commons to current stories to the effect that the whole business was a matter of collusion between the British and French Governments and the Government of Israel; and he asked the British Government to indicate the truth about this. Replying to the debate the Foreign Secretary, Mr Selwyn Lloyd, said this:

SELWYN LLOYD: The Rt Hon. Gentleman asked whether there had been collusion in regard to this matter. . . . It is quite wrong to state that Israel was incited to this action by Her Majesty's Government. There was no prior agreement between us about it. It is, of course, true that the Israeli mobilization gave some advance warning, and we urged restraint upon the Israeli Government and, in particular, drew attention to the serious consequences of any attack on Jordan. . . .[1]

The reference to Jordan was a reminder to Members of the House of Commons that Britain had a treaty with Jordan, that Israel's preparations for war had looked as though they would be directed against Jordan – not Egypt, and that Britain had informed Israel a few days earlier that it would go to the help of Jordan if it were attacked by Israel. But the questions about collusion continued, inside the Commons and out, and on 20 December 1956 the Prime Minister himself made this statement:

ANTHONY EDEN: We have been accused of being, ever since the Israeli attack on Egypt, and indeed long before that, in collusion with the Israelis. My Rt Hon. and Learned Friend the Foreign Secretary emphatically denied that charge on 31 October. Since then, it seems that the charge has been altered and Her Majesty's Government have been asked to prove that they had no foreknowledge of the Israeli attack.

[1] *Hansard.*

There were certainly a number of indications of an increasingly dangerous situation, particularly, as we thought, between Israel and Jordan. We warned the Israeli Government of the consequences of an attack on Jordan, and we gave a number of other warnings, including the general warning to which my Rt Hon. Learned Friend referred. But to say – and this is what I want to repeat to the House – that Her Majesty's Government were engaged in some dishonourable conspiracy is completely untrue, and I most emphatically deny it.[1]

Let us pause to consider the form of these denials.[2] Mr Lloyd said that Israel had not been *incited* by Britain. But incitement, as I see it, is not an essential ingredient of collusion and it was not alleged by Mr Gaitskell in his question. Mr Lloyd also denied that there was any 'prior agreement' between Britain and Israel about 'it' – 'it' presumably being the Israeli attack in Sinai.

The Prime Minister, having stated that his Government had been accused of collusion, disclaimed any 'dishonourable conspiracy'.

In his memoirs *Full Circle*[3] Lord Avon, with the access to official papers which is denied to most of the rest of us, went

---

[1] *Hansard.*

[2] At the end of the debate the Prime Minister also said:

EDEN: I want to say this on the question of foreknowledge, and to say it quite bluntly to the House, that there was not foreknowledge that Israel would attack Egypt – there was not. But there was something else. There was – we knew it perfectly well – a risk of it, and, in the event of the risk of it, certain discussions and conversations took place, as, I think, was absolutely right, and as, I think, anybody would do. So far from this being an act of retribution, I would be compelled – and I think my colleagues would agree – if I had the same very disagreeable decisions to take again, to repeat them.

Our attention was drawn to this passage by Miss Elizabeth Monroe of St Antony's College, Oxford. Both quotations from *Hansard* were broadcast in the Home Service 3 November 1966. [Ed.]

[3] *Memoirs*, by the Earl of Avon: *Full Circle* (Cassell, 1960).

very fully into some aspects of the Suez war but ignored others. Lord Avon and Mr Lloyd were of course both invited to contribute to this series of broadcasts, but they declined.[1]

So the British side of the story is thinner than I had hoped and we have to do the best we can without some of the authoritative testimony which as historians, not sensation hunters, we would have liked to have. Nevertheless you will hear some weighty witnesses. I have interviewed Lord Robens, who was shadow Foreign Secretary at the time, and one Minister who was on the very inside – Christian Pineau, the French Foreign Minister. I have also talked with two writers who have made serious and intensive studies of the subject, the Israeli Michel Bar-Zohar and the Canadian Terence Robertson; and with a Middle East expert, Jon Kimche, who has had access to important private papers and to leading participants in the affair. You will also hear the Israeli Commander-in-Chief, General Moshe Dayan, and extracts from his diary. My own comments are based on interviews with many persons over and above those who have consented to have their views made public.

The collusion controversy has centred round two meetings or alleged meetings – the first in Paris on 16 October when advisers were dispensed with and Eden and Lloyd conferred with Mollet and Pineau alone; the second on 23 and 24 October at Sèvres near Paris when an Israeli party, led by Ben-Gurion, met French Ministers and – so it is alleged – Selwyn Lloyd, after which a tripartite 'treaty' was signed.

In *Full Circle* Lord Avon[2] makes no reference at all to this later meeting. This is how he describes the earlier one:

[1] *Lord Avon referred us to his memoirs; and Mr Lloyd wrote to the producer:*
I don't think that any useful purpose could be served by my taking part in the fourth programme of your series. From time to time I have been publicly and privately asked to comment on various sensational stories. My answer has always been that I don't propose to add to what has already been said publicly about these affairs. I am afraid that I would give exactly the same answer if asked on your programme.

[2] Sir Anthony Eden had been created the Earl of Avon by the time of publication of his memoirs. I have adopted the practice of referring to him as Anthony Eden for events in 1956. [Ed.]

ANTHONY EDEN: We had to deal with three principal topics. The first was the state of general negotiations about the future of the Canal. . . . The second was the progress, if such it could be called, of the Users' Club and what our next step should be. In the third place we had to pool our information and consider the action we must take in the light of developments in the Middle East itself, and, in particular, the growing menace of hostility by Egypt against Israel.[1]

In elaborating on this third point Lord Avon points out that Israel was clearly being impelled by Fedayen raids into making some sort of military riposte, but that from the British point of view it made all the difference whether Israel attacked Britain's ally Jordan, or Egypt:

ANTHONY EDEN: To fail to carry out our engagement would be the end of our position in the Middle East, to have to carry it out would be disastrous to Western unity. No dilemma could be more difficult. If Israel were to break out against Egypt and not against Jordan, this dilemma would not arise. For this reason, if there were to be a break-out it was better from our point of view that it should be against Egypt.[2]

The Anglo-Israeli association was fated to be a markedly unequal one: Britain fought shy of any link with Israel while Israel was anxious to establish links firmly and clearly. What policies were available to Britain at the end of July 1956? Here is Elie Kedourie (see p. 75):

ELIE KEDOURIE: When the Egyptian Government nationalized the Suez Canal, there were three possible responses open to the British Government. The first was to pocket the insult and to say nothing. The second was to re-establish the British position by force, either using the British forces exclusively, or in alliance with France and nobody else. And the third was to collaborate as well with Israel, who had a quarrel with Egypt but an entirely different quarrel. One

[1] op. cit.   [2] op. cit.

short way of describing the difference between the two quar-
rels is to say that the British and the French were concerned
with the Suez Canal, whereas Israel was concerned with
Sinai. Now if it was the latter course that was to be chosen,
why is it that this was not done openly? One can only
speculate. One can say that in the whole issue of whether to
take action against Egypt or not there were a great many
difficulties confronting the Prime Minister. There was the
opposition in the country. One has the impression there was
a disunity in the Cabinet. So that a clear-cut and a resolute
plan of action was not chosen. A clear-cut and resolute plan
of action would have been to choose perhaps the second
alternative: for Britain to tackle Egypt on its own or in collaboration with France. The third alternative would also
have been clear-cut and resolute if there had been an open
alliance between the Israelis on one hand and the British and
the French on the other. But it was decided to take joint
action with Israel but take this joint action in a roundabout
manner.

The first of Professor Kedourie's three options – to forget
the insult and do nothing about the Canal – was just not on.
Even if Britain was in the mood for this which, because of the
Munich spectre and other things we have heard about in these
broadcasts, it was not, France was even less able to let the
matter go at that: this reason was the fact that the shares of the
Suez Canal Company were a popular and widespread investment with the French middle classes. The second suggestion –
for Britain to use force alone or in co-operation with France –
was what the British Government really wanted to do. But
owing to the delays imposed by Britain's defective military
machinery the third option – Anglo-French *plus* Israeli action –
apparently became in October the inevitable and logical consequence of the Franco-Israeli arrangement. As a result Britain
found itself obliged to circumvent old-established policies in
the Middle East, which it did not really want to abandon. Why?

KEDOURIE: The impression that one gets is that this was done because there was a doctrine, a powerful doctrine which dates from long before the establishment of Israel, a doctrine as to how one should deal with the Arabs or with Arab States. It seems to me that it was argued that, even though there was a quarrel with Egypt and even though a strong case could be made out that the British had the right to prosecute their quarrel with Egypt, to do so in collaboration with Israel would alienate the Arab States. I wonder whether, if that course of open collaboration with Israel had been taken, these consequences would have followed. I myself am inclined to think not. This was an open quarrel between Egypt and Britain, and the British were at liberty to take action. This could have been quite easily put across. The British were at liberty to choose whatever way seemed best to them to prosecute this quarrel. But it was thought – and this comes out by implication, particularly from Dayan's Diary of the Sinai Campaign – that there was a better prospect of ensuring the neutrality or even the sympathy of the other Arab States if, at the same time as the quarrel with Egypt was being prosecuted, Britain showed that it was just as hostile or just as unfriendly or just as lukewarm as it had ever been towards Israel. Therefore, we had the significant developments three weeks or a fortnight before the actual start of the Suez Campaign when, if Dayan's Diary is to be believed, the British were actually threatening to take action against Israel in order to help Jordan in a matter which did not really concern the Suez affair. Again we have this pretext which was ultimately resorted to, that France and Great Britain were not really concerned in the quarrel between Israel and Egypt, but were only trying to see that the peace was kept. Hence the issue of this ultimatum. On this, my short comment is that it took nobody in. It was a comedy and it seems to me that this kind of comedy does not go down well, does not really square with the status of a great power. And in Middle Eastern terms in 1956 Great Britain was still a great power. I would tend to think that in war, as Churchill put it in the epigraph to his Memoirs, the first requisite is resolution.

The Israelis, on their side, had to have British collaboration. In previous programmes we have seen how Israel was being armed by France, and Egypt by the Soviet Union. What Israel had most to fear were the Russian Ilyushin-28 bombers. What would happen if they bombed Israeli cities – especially Tel Aviv with its thousands of new arrivals, not yet steeled to the dangers of living in a besieged country like Israel. It was essential to prevent such air-raids, either by intercepting the bombers when they came, or better still by bombing their airfields so that they would never start. The alliance with France and the help of French fighter aircraft did not provide the whole answer. Israel, I am convinced, wanted British bomber support and the use of the British bases in Cyprus for operations by British or French bomber aircraft.

Mr Bar-Zohar, the Israeli author, has explained how the situation presented itself from the military and Israeli point of view:

MICHEL BAR-ZOHAR: There were two military motives. Ben-Gurion was very concerned that the Egyptian Air Force could bomb Israel and could bring disaster in the big towns in Israel – big cities like Tel Aviv, Jerusalem and Haifa. So he wanted first of all to get from the French an umbrella, a fighter cover, which would defend him from Egyptian bombers. Second, he wanted to be sure the Egyptian airfields, where all the Egyptian Air Force and Egyptian bombers were stationed, would be bombed from the air. For bombing these airfields from the air, France or Israel, or both of them, needed long-range bombers. France had no bombers at the time, and the only bombers which could do this job were the British Canberras, which could do it from Cyprus. So Ben-Gurion wanted to be sure that Britain too was going into the war, and would use its bombers for bombing the Egyptian airfields.

But this was not the only reason for Ben-Gurion's concern to make sure of Britain:

BAR-ZOHAR: Israel, and Ben-Gurion especially, was afraid that France would not go to war if the British refused to take part in it. He knew about the very close relations between France and England at the time; and he wanted to be sure that England too, not only France but also England, were going to take part in this Suez campaign. France was eager to go to this war with Israel. But during August and September there was always some reserve on the part of the British when it was a question of Israel, or even of the joint operation. You remember that Britain was not so happy about this campaign she was preparing, and that sometimes there were some signs that Britain was going to quit and not go to this war. Ben-Gurion was afraid that maybe France, if Britain decided against, would also in the last moment retreat and refuse to go into the war with Israel. This would have left Israel alone against Egypt, and against Egyptian supremacy in the air and on the ground.

Mr Kimche, the Swiss-born expert on the Middle East who speaks from close personal contact with the principal Israeli actors in this drama, puts it even more strongly:

JON KIMCHE: It was Ben-Gurion's suspicion that the British might in the event turn on the Israelis as well that brought about, I think, the tripartite collusion and the British came in. I do not think anyone any longer denies with any conviction the meeting at Sèvres where the British were represented as well.

The suspicion arose from the previous British record during the year or so before the Suez operation. There was in November 1955 an Eden proposal which would have permitted part of the Negev to go to Egypt. This was made not openly, but privately to the Egyptians. It broke down for a variety of reasons.

This was a plan apparently conceived in London during the brief Anglo-Egyptian honeymoon to achieve a settlement in the Middle East at some territorial expense to Israel. In other words by getting Israel to abandon a part of the Negev which adjoins Sinai.

Mr Kimche, who has had access to Israel's documents, went on to explain some other reasons why he is so sure Ben-Gurion was suspicious of British intentions and determined to tie the British down by a signed agreement:

KIMCHE: Much later, only a few days before the actual Suez operation, the British threatened to intervene on the side of Jordan against Israel, while the actual plan was already unfolding. There was the British refusal to allow an Israeli liaison officer to be stationed with the British troops on Cyprus for the actual operation. In fact, I believe Ben-Gurion rather suspected that the British might have bombed the Israeli troops just as they bombed the Egyptians, if they really had been too close to the Canal, in order to carry conviction; or rather in order to convince the Arabs that the British really were impartial in their intervention. He gave very strict instructions that there was not to be a soldier within the ten-mile limit when the British started bombing, so as to provide no excuse.

So much for attitudes and approaches. We come now to what actually happened. During the first half of October there was a feeling in some quarters that the moment for military action by France and Britain against the Canal had slipped by. Then, quite quickly, France and Britain concerted operations with Israel and the war began. How exactly this happened is still partly obscure. There is nothing obscure about the Franco-Israeli association which had been more or less well known for a couple of years and which I described in detail in the last programme. What is obscure is how, in October, France knit together the Israeli plan to attack in Sinai and the Anglo-French plan to attack the Canal. Monsieur Pineau has said that he told

British Ministers about Israel's intentions. He has also spoken, not without reticence, about the meeting at Sèvres which produced a tripartite treaty. Here is a passage from our conversation[1] in Paris a few weeks ago:

CHRISTIAN PINEAU: I assured them on 15 October. If you said to me at this period 'In three weeks you will invade the Canal,' my answer would be 'No'.

CALVOCORESSI: Do you choose the date 15 October for any particular reason, or is this general?

PINEAU: No, merely mid-October.

CALVOCORESSI: When the invasion actually took place, as you say, three weeks later, it was a tripartite invasion in the sense that the Anglo-French operation was preceded by some days by the Israel campaign in the Sinai Peninsula. Can you tell us at what point these two were co-ordinated?

PINEAU: That is a much more difficult question because all the opinions are not the same about it. You must understand that Israel did not say to us: we have the intention to invade the Sinai. We did nothing. But Israel said to the French first: we have the firm intention to invade the Sinai. What will you do?

CALVOCORESSI: Can I ask you when they said this? Roughly speaking?

PINEAU: I don't remember exactly the date. . . .

CALVOCORESSI: Some time before the event.

PINEAU: Yes, in October.

CALVOCORESSI: Yes, in October.

PINEAU: In October. And personally at this period I went to London and I said to Eden, 'There is the question of Israel, what will you do?' And Eden said, 'We have to discuss this question together' and we discussed this question, and we discussed this question with Israel, the Israeli Government. And for the English, if my opinion is true, for the English the English Government had two preoccupations. First:

[1] Recorded 31 May 1966.

protect the Canal against the Egyptian Government; and was: against the Israeli Government. This point explains this extraordinary ultimatum of the Anglo-French Government, an ultimatum not very clear. And that was the point of view, the attitude of the English Government. For us the problem of the Canal was very important. And the second problem was the protection of Israel against the possibility of Russian or any external aid to Egypt. We were absolutely sure that if we destroyed the Egyptian – *la flotte* . . .

CALVOCORESSI: The air force . . .

PINEAU: The air force yes. I thought it was. If you destroyed the Egyptian Air Force it were not possible to have an extension of the conflict. It was an opinion. And our points of view were not absolutely the same.

CALVOCORESSI: No. But in general this question of an Israeli element in an attack on Egypt arose about the middle of October, and was discussed by you with British Ministers. Now at what point were the arrangements formalized? Is it possible to say, having discussed these matters of co-ordination, which had now become tripartite, at what point they were formalized?

PINEAU: The definite arrangements between the French, the English and the Israelis were made about 24, 25 October, during a special meeting.

CALVOCORESSI: A special meeting where?

PINEAU: That is another question. For the present time we have not to discuss circumstances of this meeting because all the opinions are not the same about this question.

CALVOCORESSI: Well, I quite understand that if there are different views about certain things, you do not want to discuss them any further. But am I right in saying this: that there was a special meeting, and it did take place and that is as far as you wish to go at the present time?

PINEAU: Yes. Personally I was present, Mr Ben-Gurion was present, and that is all.

CALVOCORESSI: That's all you want to say?

PINEAU: Yes, that's all.

CALVOCORESSI: Could I just add one slight point to this? Of course there has been a great deal of secrecy and one understands that there often is a great deal of secrecy about things that go on in the diplomatic world. It has never been clear to me why, at any rate from the French point of view, there was any need for secrecy. Was there from the French point of view a great need for secrecy at this time?

PINEAU: It was absolutely necessary for everybody to have the secret in this period. A treaty like the Anglo-French-Israeli Treaty was necessarily secret, because the circumstances were very difficult. And I think maybe after ten years it would be possible to say more, and if one day my English friends of this period accept to say all the truths about this question, I should agree.

A secret 'Anglo-French-Israeli Treaty'... contents still secret – existence not so secret. This is of course the meeting – or, as some people would have it, non-meeting – which took place at Sèvres.

Clearly something happened. M. Pineau's account brings Britain, France and Israel together, in place and time, at least once. Details we still do not have. But there are people who do not believe that this can have happened at all.

Lord Robens was the Labour Party spokesman on Foreign Affairs throughout the Suez crisis. I asked him his views on the secret meeting and secret treaty to which M. Pineau refers:

LORD ROBENS: Well, I do not know whether there were any face-to-face meetings with Israeli Ministers. I do not really believe that there was any formal agreement made as to what action the British should take in the event of this disturbance over the Gaza strip. But I do believe that the French and the British had agreed as to what they would both do in the event of such an eventuality. If, in fact, there were any meetings with the Israeli Ministers subsequently, I do not believe that the Israelis would have dealt with the same candour and frankness with the British as they had obviously dealt with the French. In other words, I believe the French and the Israelis were absolutely in accord on these events. And that in point of fact Eden and Lloyd were duped by the French and found themselves involved in arrangements which subsequently turned out so disastrously.

The outstanding feature of tripartite co-operation when it actually took place was the British bombing of Egyptian airfields. I asked Lord Robens if he knew anything at the time which would explain how this came about. He replied by drawing on the experiences he had gained during a visit to the Middle East at the beginning of 1956:

ROBENS: The story goes back to the build-up of arms by the Egyptians on the Gaza strip. It was very well known to those who were close enough to the situation that the Israelis were contemplating a defensive war. I was made aware of this in January of that year, and conveyed this information to the appropriate quarters which included Selwyn Lloyd and Anthony Eden. I believe that the French and the British discussed the possibility of a defensive war by the Israelis, and that they came to an agreement or some arrangements about what they would both do in the event of it happening. And I believe that when it did happen that action which the British had decided they would do was carried out. But I do not believe that the British and the Israelis actually conspired together in connection with the incident at the Gaza strip.

CALVOCORESSI: Did you, too, in your discussions with British Ministers, with Eden and Lloyd, did you discuss what in fact you would have done yourself, if you had been Foreign Secretary instead of Shadow Foreign Secretary?

ROBENS: Well yes, of course we did. This was the whole thing that concerned us very much indeed. You see, there was a very solemn treaty that had been drawn up to meet such an eventuality as this. After the war in the Middle East between the Arabs and Israel there was an armistice which settled the frontiers, and the tripartite agreement of 1950 provided for two very important things. It provided for action if the frontiers were violated, and it provided for the control of arms. Now the provision for violation of the frontier was, that if it happened, Britain, America and France should consult together as to the action to be taken. And from my point of view, and indeed from the [Labour] Party's point of view, what we were saying was, 'Here you have an agreement to meet this eventuality. Carry out the tripartite agreement.' This was the whole gravamen of our charge against the Government of the day in relation to Suez: that they had a solemn agreement to take certain action in the event of certain events taking place; this they did not do, but relied upon decisions that they had made secretly between the French and themselves. This, in my view, was the line that the Government should have taken. If in fact they had taken this line there would have been no problem with the Americans, and there would have been a proper solution to this whole very unhappy and, I am afraid, sordid affair.

CALVOCORESSI: From your conversations with Ministers were you expecting right up to the last moment that the British Government would consult with the United States?

ROBENS: I happened to be dining at Downing Street on the evening when the Israelis invaded Egypt, and the note which was passed to Anthony Eden was passed to Selwyn Lloyd and subsequently passed to me. I remember it very clearly. It said that the Israelis had invaded Egypt and were seventy miles inside Egyptian territory. The meal was towards its close and as soon as coffee was to be served Eden asked me to step on one side with him, which I did, and we had a very close conversation. During that conversation he indicated how important it was that there should be unity of the parties in an issue of this kind, and I agreed that this was very important. I then said that obviously he would now bring into effect the tripartite agreement and that very obviously discussions with the French and the Americans should take place immediately. He was somewhat confused at this stage, and neither agreed nor disagreed but merely went on to say how important it was that the nation should not be divided on this issue. Now when in the House of Commons subsequently he made his statement I was perhaps more surprised than any man in England that he had taken the line that he had.

When I left Downing Street that night I was convinced in my own mind that the obvious thing would be done, and that was to put the tripartite agreement into effect, and that meant consultation with America and France.

The Prime Minister's statement referred to by Lord Robens was his report to the House of Commons on the ultimatum delivered by Britain and France to Israel and Egypt. It is of course quite normal in this country for Opposition Leaders to be in close private contact with Ministers when something especially important is going on. Eden was evidently much concerned about national unity, and off the record he got from Lord Robenr a direct account of what the Labour Party was thinking. But it seems to me that maybe Lord Robens was not treated so frankly in return.

In an inquiry like the one we are engaged in in these broadcasts one naturally begins with the politicians, but as time goes by other people find out things too. The writers and researchers get going. Much the most detailed account of this final episode before the war began has been given by Terence Robertson in his book, *Crisis: the inside story of the Suez conspiracy*.[1] Mr Robertson spent two to three years trying to unravel the Suez conundrum, and the part played by Canada during the rescue operation. He interviewed dozens of people from Cabinet Ministers downwards. I asked Mr Robertson how he came to be able to set down such a detailed account of especially secret meetings:

[1] Hutchinson, 1965.

ROBERTSON: I believe that the French leaders I spoke to, having no motives really for hiding anything, having no real reason to evade anything, were frank when I asked them questions; and indeed not only frank but quite pleased and proud of what they had done. Therefore, when M. Pineau, for instance, gave me his statement on everything that had happened from the time he took office until the Suez event itself, I believed that he was giving a very frank and full account. He traced the events that led to the meetings after the nationalization of the Canal. He made it perfectly clear that he and Bourgès-Maunoury[1] were to a large extent the architects of the concept of collusion mainly because their leader, their premier, M. Mollet, would not do anything without British support. So in order to establish some sort of action against Colonel Nasser they had to bring Britain in. And Pineau made this his responsibility. He explained how this happened.

I subsequently went to M. Bourgès-Maunoury and confronted him with all that M. Pineau had said, and he confirmed every detail of it. And this led, of course, right through to the meeting with Ben-Gurion and Selwyn Lloyd at Sèvres, on I think it was 23 October 1956. M. Mollet confirmed as well that he had met Ben-Gurion. He was unsure of the dates but M. Bourgès-Maunoury and M. Pineau were not; they were quite clear on the dates. They were quite clear that Ben-Gurion, Peres[2] and Dayan[3] with their staffs, arrived by French aircraft at approximately seven or eight o'clock in the morning of the 23rd, and that there were talks all that day between Pineau and Mollet and Ben-Gurion: that Selwyn Lloyd arrived in the late afternoon, or early evening, with Sir Patrick Dean, who was then Assistant Under-Secretary at the Foreign Office; that Selwyn Lloyd and Dean were briefed on all that had gone on during the day. It was agreed

---

[1] French Defence Minister.
[2] Director-General of the Israeli Ministry of Defence.
[3] Israeli Commander-in-Chief.

that, in the event that the Israelis felt bound to go through with their attack in the Sinai, which they had decided to do, the French were quite right to cover their cities with airplanes and protect their coast with ships; and that the British would, in fact, be not concerned so much with the defence of Israel, but with keeping the Egyptian Air Force from flying. Selwyn Lloyd returned that night to England, reported to Anthony Eden, I think, at ten o'clock that night at Downing Street – this is the timing once again given by Pineau and by Bourgès-Maunoury – and the following morning Patrick Dean was authorized from London to agree to the detailed terms. On the third day a treaty was drawn up, three copies – one for Israel, one for France, and one for Britain. Ben-Gurion signed for Israel, Pineau for France and Patrick Dean for Britain.

CALVOCORESSI: This seems an extremely circumstantial story, full of detail, and is it true to say that it comes almost entirely from French sources?

ROBERTSON: Yes, except that when I went to Israel I put this whole thing to the Foreign Minister at the time, Mrs Golda Meir, and to Ben-Gurion. They would not elaborate, and so I asked them whether they would in fact deny it; and they said 'No'.

Mr Robertson mentioned Sir Patrick Dean and I feel there is something I ought to say about this. Sir Patrick Dean was a Civil Servant. He still is a Civil Servant. He is our Ambassador in Washington at the present time. So by the rules we have in this country he cannot be expected to comment on anything that is said about his participation in these affairs. It was simply his job to go there to do whatever he was told to do and to keep quiet about it afterwards.

Mr Bar-Zohar's independent researches led him to the same general conclusion. I should interject here that Mr Bar-Zohar is Ben-Gurion's official biographer. I asked him whether Israel's Prime Minister got what he wanted when he flew to France.

BAR-ZOHAR: Yes. Ben-Gurion got his famous Treaty which was signed at Sèvres, after the conference which lasted for about three days, and where French and British Ministers took part. At the end of this conference there were three protocols signed – one for France, one for England and one for Israel. As you know during the Suez war Israel got its famous umbrella from French jet fighters, which were Mystères, and even I think, yes, there were some Sabres: they had not even removed the NATO colours from them. On the other hand the British bombed the Egyptian airfields with Canberras.

CALVOCORESSI: And you say this was put into a formal agreement on paper and signed.

BAR-ZOHAR: Yes, it was put.

CALVOCORESSI: Now we have been told by M. Pineau that he himself was present at this famous meeting. What other French Ministers were there? Pineau was, of course, the Foreign Minister at the time.

BAR-ZOHAR: Pineau was the Foreign Minister. There was also Guy Mollet of course – who was Prime Minister – and he took part, a very active part, in this conference. And there was also, I think, the most important man from the French side which was Maurice Bourgès-Maunoury. He was Minister of Defence. He was the force which pushed all the time for making this war. There were also some French generals, very important, like General Challe and some others.

CALVOCORESSI: He was French Chief of Staff, Challe?

BAR-ZOHAR: He was Chief of Staff, yes. From the Israelis, there were Ben-Gurion, Shimon Peres, General Dayan, and some of their aides. From the British side, there was Selwyn Lloyd and Mr Patrick Dean, who is now the British representative in the United Nations.

CALVOCORESSI: He is British Ambassador in Washington.

BAR-ZOHAR: That's it.

Even if we knew nothing at all about the meeting at Sèvres

and the 'Treaty of Sèvres' – which, as you see, is very far from being the case – we might still deduce some measure of Anglo-French-Israeli consultation, at the very least, from what happened when the war began. Here are some entries in the diary of General Dayan, Israeli Commander-in-Chief:

DAYAN DIARIES: *25 October* – After numerous internal conferences, and contacts and clarifications with people overseas, which started about two months ago, we can sum up the situation today as follows:

1. The Prime Minister and Minister of Defence, David Ben-Gurion, has given approval in principle to the campaign and its aims.
2. Our forces will go into action at dusk on 29 October 1956, and we must complete the capture of the Sinai Peninsula within seven to ten days.
3. The decisions on the campaign and its planning are based on the assumption that British and French forces are about to take action against Egypt.
4. According to information in our possession, the Anglo-French forces propose to launch their operations on 31 October 1956. Their aim is to secure control of the Suez Canal Zone, and for this they will need to effect a sea landing or an air drop with, no doubt, suitable air cover.

At 13.45 I met with the senior officers of Operation Branch. . . . I transmitted what I could of the political conditions within the framework of which we would be conducting our campaign. From the operational point of view we had to distinguish between the period up to the start of the Anglo-French action and the period after. It may be assumed that with the launching of their attack, the Egyptian Air Force will cease its activity against us. Egyptian Army units in Sinai will almost certainly be ordered to withdraw into Egypt, and those remaining in their positions will find their morale lowered. Therefore what it may be possible to

do after the Anglo-French assault we need not try to do
before.

26 October – The Navy were disappointed that their tasks
do not include operations in the Mediterranean; but it is our
assumption that Anglo-French vessels will tie down the
Egyptian Navy, and we must apply our naval strength to the
Red Sea. Moreover, activity on our part in the Mediterranean
without co-ordination with the Anglo-French forces is likely
to lead to mishaps.[1]

These extracts do not by themselves prove any far-reaching
agreement, and the last one in fact shows that any agreement
there may have been was certainly not worked out in any detail.

General Dayan was himself in London a few days ago[2] and
I took the opportunity to ask him how far his plan for the Sinai
campaign was based on foreknowledge of an Anglo-French
attack on Egypt.

GENERAL DAYAN: Well, I should say the entire military plan
was based on that.

CALVOCORESSI: What difference would it have made to you if
you had had no such foreknowledge?

DAYAN: Well, we would have then taken care to gain air
superiority on the Egyptians before we could have committed our infantry forces going in the naked desert.

CALVOCORESSI: When you say that you based your plans on
foreknowledge, does this include foreknowledge of times
and dates?

DAYAN: Yes. We assumed and we thought that we knew. As
a matter of fact, later on it turned out that the Anglo-French
forces did not start on that date when we expected them to
do so.

In point of fact the Israelis' information was not wrong.
What happened was that the Anglo-French operation was
delayed at the last moment. Nevertheless I put it to General

[1] Dayan, op. cit., pp. 60–1, 66–7.
[2] Recorded 11 July 1966.

Dayan that Israel had made a slight mistake in the timing of its attack in Sinai:

DAYAN: We were wrong in our assumption, and we were very worried about this.

CALVOCORESSI: How much then did you know in advance about British and French plans?

DAYAN: Well, we knew that they were about to occupy the Suez Canal Zone, and I should say – well, that's ten years ago! – that we knew more or less about, or we thought that we knew more or less about the general size of their forces, and they were going to start by an air attack. That was a combination of knowledge and assumption.

CALVOCORESSI: When you say an air attack do you mean an air attack on the Canal or an air attack on Egyptian airfields?

DAYAN: On Egyptian airfields.

CALVOCORESSI: And how important was this for you?

DAYAN: Oh, it was terribly important because otherwise I should say that *we* had to start that way. One cannot in a desert warfare really commit infantry forces without, I should say, gaining a major amount of air superiority earlier.

Then there comes the question of the Anglo-French ultimatum to Israel and Egypt. This, as we heard in the first programme, was delivered on 30 October and required both Israel and Egypt to retire from the Canal. Lord Avon gives an account of why this ultimatum was delivered:

ANTHONY EDEN: On 25 October a report came that Israel was about to mobilize. She did so on the 27th and moved against Egypt on the evening of the 29th.

The chief peril to us lay not in the conflict but in its extension by the intervention of other Arab States. The best way to halt that was by intervening ourselves.

Our purpose was to safeguard free passage through the Canal, if it were threatened with becoming a zone of warfare, and to arrest the spread of fighting in the Middle East.

To realize this we would put into operation the plan for occupation of the Suez Canal zone, prepared by the joint Anglo-French military staff which had been studying the problem since the end of July. An advantage of this course was that we did not need to recast our military preparations. The same plan that had been intended to deal with Nasser's seizure of the Canal fitted equally well with our new objective. Critics asked why we landed so far behind the combatant area. The answer is that to land anywhere except as planned would have involved delay and we could not afford delay. We were also limited by shortage of landing craft and had to have the use of a port.[1]

On the very same day when the British Cabinet, according to Lord Avon, was making the decision to meet the risks of Israeli action by putting into effect the Anglo-French plan to occupy the Canal – on that very day General Dayan was already assuming, as we have just heard, that Britain and France were about to take action against Egypt. Each of them – Britain and Israel – seems to have felt sure that the other was about to act.

In any case the Israelis treated the ultimatum as bogus. General Dayan noted:

DAYAN DIARY: This ultimatum does not worry Israel. We are not within ten miles of the Canal and we have neither interest nor plan to come closer to it. It is clear that the whole purpose of the ultimatum is to give the British and French Governments a pretext to capture the Canal Zone by military force. Doubtless the Egyptians will not willingly agree to the conditions of the ultimatum, and particularly to the Anglo-French occupation of key positions in the Zone.[2]

Again, it cannot in my view be argued from the ultimatum alone that there was the sort of collusion we have been talking about. What the ultimatum shows is something more general: that things were not what they seemed, that somebody

[1] *Full Circle*, op. cit.   [2] Dayan, op. cit., p. 97.

was concerned to practise deceit. André Fontaine calls it a 'disappointing' way to behave:

FONTAINE: I think one of the most disappointing facts about all this time is the way the ultimatum was given both by Britain and by France, which tried to make believe that France and Great Britain had really no other purpose than to separate the Israelis and the Egyptians who were about to make a war on the Suez Canal. I think this was something very cynical, because at that same time there had been military agreements between France and Israel and through France between Britain and Israel.

We are left with a number of 'ifs' and 'buts'. Yet *is* it so difficult to stand back, take a cool look at the essentials and come out with a forthright judgement? Mr Kimche proposed to do so:

KIMCHE: Well, there was quite a lot of sort of contrived diplomacy on all sides, at that time. It was almost fashionable as between, say, the Egyptians and the Russians, the French and the Israelis, the French and the British. But hardly the British and the Israelis! But I think, or at least I would say I know, that in the event there was an arrangement. And there was also an undertaking that nothing would be said about this, certainly for the classic fifty-year period, if then. And the Israelis, Mr Ben-Gurion himself and his successor, have always taken a firm stand with any budding memoir writer who wanted to reveal the full story, or with anyone else.

What is the historical importance of collusion? In terms of Israel or of France I would say very little. The Israelis agreed to keep quiet about the arrangements that were made because without this promise they would not have got the arrangements. The French, who were the principal engineers of the deal, also kept quiet because keeping quiet was a necessary condition of achieving their aims vis-à-vis their associates, the other governments with whom they were negotiating the arrangements. Both the French and the Israeli governments promised secrecy in order to get something out of Britain. But Britain's position was different.

I said at the beginning, and I want to repeat, that there is nothing wrong about secrecy. A great deal of international discussion goes on in secret and must. The question one has to exercise is whether, in any given case, the motives for secrecy are valid. In the Suez case Britain's motives must – until the relevant Cabinet papers are made available – be taken to be these:

First, to deceive the other Arabs who must not be allowed to think that Britain could associate with Israel. We have heard Professor Kedourie's view that if Britain had proceeded openly in its quarrel with Nasser about the Canal, these Arabs would not have taken Nasser's side.

Second, to keep the United States in the dark because otherwise the Americans might have thwarted the Anglo-French operation – for example, by using the Sixth Fleet to get in the way.

Third, by keeping some Members of the British Government itself in the dark, to avoid a major dramatic political row which could have brought the Government down. The Cabinet was certainly divided, but the opposition within it was virtually nullified by pretences.

Finally, to hide things from the British public which, as the event proved, was anything but united over Suez, in spite of the normal tendency to close ranks in war.

Therefore, if there was collusion as I have defined it – and I personally have become convinced that the evidence supports the charge – then British Ministers deceived their friends in the Arab world, their principal ally, their Ministerial colleagues and their public.

5. Political Echoes

by ROBERT RHODES JAMES
introduced by PETER CALVOCORESSI

First broadcast 14 July 1966[1]

PETER CALVOCORESSI: *In the first four programmes I have tried to recall the historical background; to explain the position of Egypt and then of Israel before, during and since the war; and to probe in particular Britain's association with Israel. These programmes have inevitably left certain topics on one side and it is to these that we turn in the second half of this series. We begin with the political consequences in this country – the effects on the politicians themselves and on the political climate right down to today. We asked a political biographer and historian to do this job and we chose one who is himself a member of the Suez generation – who date their interest in politics from 1956. Mr Robert Rhodes James has written biographies of Lord Randolph Churchill[2] and Lord Rosebery[3] and a history of Gallipoli.[4] He is now a Fellow of All Souls College, Oxford:*

ROBERT RHODES JAMES: Munich provided me with my first political experience. I was five years old, and my parents – on leave from India – had rented a flat in Earl's Court Road over a butcher's shop. One reached it by means of a staircase which always seemed to me a mile long, and down which I fell helter-skelter on one occasion. We had a small but comfortable drawing-room, and one evening I bounced gaily into it to say goodnight to my parents. To my surprise I was emphatically 'shushed' by the grown-ups, who were listening anxiously to the wireless. An old man was talking about a con-

[1] Under the title *Constitutional Echoes*.
[2] *Lord Randolph Churchill*, Weidenfeld & Nicolson (1959).
[3] *Rosebery*, Weidenfeld & Nicolson (1963).
[4] *Gallipoli*, Batsford (1965).

flict in 'a far-away country between people of whom we know nothing'. That was my first recollection of Munich and Neville Chamberlain. I also remember, when out with my nanny in Kensington Gardens, seeing the beautiful silver barrage balloons rising over London, and I accompanied my mother on some of her expeditions to instruct unwilling victims in the horrors of the gas-mask.

It seems inevitable, when one thinks of Suez, to cast one's mind back to Munich, for the intense passions that Suez aroused had not been seen in this country since the autumn of 1938. It could be said of Suez, as Sir Winston Churchill has written of Munich:

> Families and friends in intimate contact were divided to a degree the like of which I have never seen. Men and women long bound together by party ties, social amenities, and family connections, glared upon one another in scorn and anger.

My memories of Suez are peculiarly vivid. I was, at the time, one of the Clerks of the House of Commons, and had literally a front-row seat in the gallery as the long drama unfolded. In August 1956 I got married, and spent part of my honeymoon in Oxford. One glittering morning we walked from Iffley along the towpath – that exquisite walk – into the city, to see what seemed an endless procession of sand-coloured lorries and armoured cars proceeding southwards. It was a spectacle both impressive and chilling on that beautiful summer morning.

It is important to recall that there were in fact two Suez crises. The first erupted at the end of July, when Nasser nationalized the Canal. I well remember the mood of the House on the next morning, a sunny Friday. There was not a dissenting voice. This mood of unanimous resolve continued throughout the following week. The House rose for the Summer Recess having given the Government full support for firm and vigorous action. But as the weeks passed, this mood changed. When Parliament met briefly in September to debate the situation, the shift of opinion in the Labour Party was very apparent. When the second and major crisis came in October, the storm really broke. The contrast between the mood of the House of Commons in July and that in October was indeed dramatic. No one who lived through those wild days of storm and tumult will ever forget the Suez debates. Only the wise experience and meticulous skill of the Speaker, the late W. S. Morrison (Lord Dunrossil), averted an even more serious clash. There were moments when it seemed inevitable that the House would dissolve in complete disorder. It was, as anyone who was there will testify, a very close thing.

These facts are important, for they partly explain one of the phenomena of Suez – the surprisingly small short-term political effects on the Conservative Government. The slump in the reputation of Sir Anthony Eden was due not so much to Suez itself as to the subsequent withdrawal, and, most unfairly, to his brief period of recuperation in Jamaica. But Eden's reputation among his own supporters had been slithering downward for many months before Suez; indeed the events of August–November actually restored it. Like Rosebery, he had acquired that most melancholy of political epithets – *capex imperii nisi imperasset*.

It was said of Munich that no one supported it – in retrospect. The same could be said of Suez. At the time a great many people supported it. I remember that several Labour M.P.s returned from a weekend visit to their constituencies at the height of the crisis extremely thoughtful. A friend who worked in the London docks reported a thoroughly belligerent spirit in that sector. Public Opinion Polls, although not so widely relied upon in 1956 as today, seem to confirm what was certainly my impression at the time, that a majority – albeit a small one – of the nation supported the Government's Suez policy. Much of this support, I suspect, was on the 'my country right or wrong' principle; some, alas, was based on xenophobia.

But it is important to remember that this support existed. As Mr Henry Pelling, the historian of the Labour Party, has written: 'There was a strong feeling of popular jingoism which was evident even among regular Labour supporters.' Looked at from the outside, the attitude of the Labour Party was somewhat difficult to understand. It had supported the military preparations in August, and, apart from talking vaguely about referring the dispute to the United Nations, it made no positive proposal throughout the following three months. If the Labour Party was unalterably opposed to the use of force against Nasser, it was argued, why had it supported the original military preparations? To such questions the Labour Party vanished in a cloud of vague generalities. To outsiders, it seemed very reminiscent of the thirties, when the cry was collective security without rearmament. It now seemed to be: to prepare for military action but not to take it.

Then there was the personal contribution of Hugh Gaitskell. It is difficult for me to speak objectively about him, for I had a high personal regard for him and lament his untimely death profoundly. But I am sure it will be the verdict of history that he cut an unimpressive figure in the whole Suez story. His famous – or perhaps, notorious – television broadcast, in which he appealed to the Conservative Party to throw Eden over, was appallingly maladroit. And, in spite of the qualifications in his first Commons speech on the nationalization of the Canal, which were subsequently blown up out of all proportion to explain his apparent *volte face*, the fact was that he had firmly supported the Government in the early – and crucial – stages of the 'first' Suez Crisis. 'It is all very familiar,' he had said on 2 August. 'It is exactly the same that we encountered from Mussolini and Hitler.' He had, in short, hitched the Labour Party to Sir Anthony Eden's wagon, and it proved to be very difficult to unhitch it without looking ridiculous – or something a good deal worse.

Above all – and this, I feel, was the vital factor – it seemed as though the Labour leader was not leading his Party, but was being himself led – and led by the Left. This was unfair; but the imputation of indecision was there and it left its mark.

Indeed it was not until Gaitskell turned on the Labour Left over unilateralism in 1960 that he emerged as a really national figure. The British love a fighter, in politics as in anything else. For years they failed to detect the steel in Gaitskell's complex and puzzling personality. But one really cannot blame them for not seeing it at Suez.

Thus it was that the Labour Party was in popular estimation very much *parti pris* over Suez. And the very violence of its reaction to the news of the Anglo-French ultimatum in October revived one of the most potent of all Tory allegations – that the Labour Party is the Unpatriotic Party. There were many people who were appalled at the ultimatum and appalled by the invasion, but who believed that national unity must be preserved when British troops are going into action, and, at the very least, that there must be some sense of proportion.

It was, I think, the note of shrill hysteria in the opposition to the Government that really did the damage. If the proceedings of the House of Commons had been televised, the feeling of public revulsion would have been even greater than it was. The booing and screaming started whenever Eden entered the Chamber, and it went on from there. And it was a significant moment when Eden – prematurely, and probably disastrously – announced the surrender of Port Said. The Labour uproar vanished into a ghastly, sickly silence, and the Government benches erupted in delight.

In these circumstances it was not difficult to pin the ancient label of 'The Unpatriotic Party' on the Labour movement. It seemed to me that only the late Aneurin Bevan kept his head. His performances in the debates revealed how wantonly the Labour Party had thrown away its advantages by the manner of its opposition. In the event, they made almost every mistake of tactics and strategy that a political confederation could have made.

It is axiomatic of politics that no party must be seen to be what its opponents allege it to be. The Tories must struggle not to be seen to be the 'Party of the Bosses.' The Labour Party must take care that it is not convicted of being 'The Un-patriotic Party'.

These factors, I believe, help to explain why it was that Mr Macmillan was able to drag the Conservative Party out of the depths of the post-Suez disillusionment in 1957 to the electoral triumph of 1959. And it was also significant that Suez played a very minor part in the 1959 Election. I am sure that Lord Kilmuir was right when he wrote that: 'If Suez was remembered at all in the 1959 election, it was the Labour Party that suffered.'

There were several extremely significant *personal* consequences. Only two Ministers – Sir Edward Boyle and Mr Anthony Nutting – resigned, although it is thought that Sir Walter Monckton's resignation from the Ministry of Defence just before the crisis was connected with his views on Government policy – but this is still conjecture. Only two members of Parliament – Mr Nigel Nicolson (Conservative) and Mr Stanley Evans (Labour) – were disowned by their constituency associations as a direct result of opposing their Party's attitude over Suez, although some others – mainly Conservatives who were critical of the Government – found themselves in serious trouble with their constituency associations. Mr Nigel Nicolson had been on uneasy terms with his constituency association before Suez: Mr Stanley Evans resigned his seat and retired from public life. There were many people who regretted that he did not contest the right of a constituency association to tell an M.P. what his attitude should be on a matter of major national importance of this kind. Mr Nicolson did so, but he lost.

But the real personal consequences were at a higher level. It is, I think, evident to all who were in the Commons at the time that Mr Butler, by appearing to be attempting to be all things to all men, wrecked what chances he had of the succession to Sir Anthony Eden. The professional political commentators who in January 1957 tipped him so confidently for the Premiership must have been walking the Whitehall and Westminster corridors with their eyes closed and with their ears plugged.

E

Mr Randolph Churchill may or may not have had inside information when he, virtually alone, forecast Mr Macmillan's accession to 'Elijah's Mantle'; but inside information was not necessary. Even I, a very young and wholly inexperienced observer, had no doubts; luckily I put them on paper in a private letter to a friend, so I have documentary proof.

It is, of course, uncertain whether Mr Butler would have succeeded Sir Anthony Eden if there had been no Suez crisis; but I have no doubt whatever that the crisis destroyed what chances Mr Butler had. This seems to me to be an indisputable fact. Mr Butler may have been unfairly treated, but Suez really destroyed him as surely as it destroyed Sir Anthony Eden. Mr Macmillan's part may have been Machiavellian; but it was certainly highly effective. It was during the Suez crisis that he definitely emerged as the serious contender for the leadership in the event of Sir Anthony Eden's retirement. Eden's health had been poor for some time before the Suez crisis broke; although during it, at least in the Commons, he maintained an aura of supreme confidence, and, most remarkably, his hold on the House. It seems clear that the immense strain of the crisis accelerated his retirement, and it is a fact that the course of the crisis determined his successor.

The crisis also played a vital part in the career of another Conservative politician – Mr Edward Heath, the Chief Whip. The publicity given to the right-wing so-called 'Suez Group' has tended to obscure the fact that there were several other Conservatives who were deeply troubled over the Government's action; although few in number, their defection could have brought the Government down. And, although few in number, this group contained some influential Members. Perhaps more than any other single man, Mr Heath held the Party together during the critical forty-eight hours following the ultimatum. Even before Suez he was being hailed as one of the best Chief Whips of modern times; Suez amply confirmed this view, and raised his reputation on all sides to new heights.

This success was the starting point of his subsequent rise to the leadership of the Party in 1965.

Suez, like Gallipoli, was a great destroyer of reputations – military as well as political. It is often forgotten that it made others. The new Toryism that Mr Macmillan created between 1957 and 1960 was born out of the post-Suez shambles. The very severity of the crisis made the Party amenable to changes which, in quiet times, would have been more strenuously opposed. This was particularly – and most dramatically – evident in colonial policy. Mr Macmillan achieved the apparently impossible. He transformed party policy over a wide field, at home and abroad; he gave opportunities to new and younger men, he restored the situation abroad, particularly with the United States; and he succeeded in reviving the Conservatives' will to win – that undefinable but crucial factor in a political party's fortunes after a great reverse.

The bold stand of the Labour Party against aggression had been compromised by the various factors I have referred to. Mr Ivor Bulmer-Thomas, in his recent study of the British Party System, has written that 'the effect of Suez on the Labour Party was to give it a sense of unity, purpose and confidence that it had not known for six years'. This may have been true of the feeling in the crisis itself, but the unity – as we know – was short lived. Indeed, the Party clearly found itself in a considerable difficulty when it was all over. In the complicated months following Suez it seemed unable to make up its mind on its future course. It certainly, in modern parlance, let the Government 'off the hook'. The Opposition seemed to be more emotionally exhausted after the crisis than the Government. Public opinion polls and by-elections showed a steady swing back to the Government in 1958 and 1959. The Parliamentary Session of 1958–59 was almost eerily peaceful for a pre-election Session.

Above all, the Labour Party seemed increasingly uneasy about exploiting Suez, no doubt believing that this might rebound to its disadvantage. Perhaps this apprehension was justified and was wise. It was only after the advent of Mr Wilson in 1963 that one began to hear 'Suez' referred to at length by Labour leaders in attacks on the Conservative record from 1951 onwards.

If, as I believe, the short-term effects of Suez on the British political scene were surprisingly small, the long-term consequences were of immense significance. I have compared Suez to Munich in the passions it aroused. Perhaps one might also remember the Spanish Civil War. For it was among the young – particularly at the universities – that Suez had such profound effect. Eden's frequent references to Hitler and the re-militarization of the Rhineland had effect on the over-forties; none on the under-thirties. There was an explosion – and I do not think it too strong a word – among students. Oxford, when I was up between 1952 and 1955, was passing through a somewhat Conservative phase. But it was a period primarily of very little feeling of political involvement. Suez changed all that. Many supporters of the Labour Party who are now in their early thirties, coming from backgrounds which are not predominantly Labour, trace their conversion – or, rather, their awakening of political involvement – to Suez. The revulsion against the Macmillan Government between 1961 and 1963 among members of this generation – my generation – has I think been wrongly ascribed to 'You never had it so good'; it was more complicated than that; it was, I believe, a revulsion against the kind of cynicism that was typified by Suez. There can be few people who do not now believe that there was collusion between Great Britain, France and Israel. This was the final disillusionment.

These feelings were greatly augmented by what had happened almost simultaneously in Hungary. Here were two examples of the old kind of brute diplomacy – different only in degree. The cumulative effect was very profound.

Thus it was that in the long run Suez came home to roost on the Tory Party. The passions faded away, but the feelings that had aroused those passions did not. Suez has bitten itself deeply into my generation. The Conservative Party will have to wait for many years before the shadow of Suez ceases to darken its good repute. If this is rough justice, justice, in politics, is usually pretty rough. But it is justice all the same.

6. Meanwhile in Hungary

by JOHN ERICKSON
introduced by PETER CALVOCORESSI

First broadcast 25 July 1966

PETER CALVOCORESSI: *One of the topics which we cannot ignore in this series is the Hungarian Revolution and how the Russians suppressed it. Did Hungary affect Suez or vice versa? Dr John Erickson of Manchester University, who is our leading specialist in Soviet military affairs, has made a special study of the available evidence. I shall be adding a comment or two of my own at the end.*

JOHN ERICKSON: Even after the lapse of ten years, the hurt to the Western conscience at having been a mere spectator to the destruction of the Hungarian Revolution by Soviet military intervention is still very quick. The revulsion was expressed in the wave of frantic demonstrations in November 1956 and, in another wave of soul-searching, the European Communist parties were hit by mass defection and resignation, all expressions of dismay and disgust at the Soviet action. The anguish in the West, however, went deeper at the thought that the Anglo-French intervention at Suez had either provided the occasion for the drastic Soviet blow at Hungary, or at the very least had made it impossible for any aid to be rendered to the embattled Hungarians. When the first numbing shock had worn off, it was replaced by a nagging sense of the fatal causality between Suez and Hungary, or by addition to hypotheses – *if* the Israeli attack had come a month later, or *if* the Anglo-French ultimatum had come later, Hungary would have been spared its horrors, or indeed any permutation of time with circumstance in that whole feverish month.

Ten years ago, with passions roused and the blood fresh spilt, with conscience torn between condemnation and self-immolation, there was no time in which fact might superim-

118

pose itself upon assumption. Ten years later, it is easier to lay the whole question across the chopping-block of chronology, though to test it against history in the absolute sense remains even now impossible owing to the lack of direct evidence relating to Soviet decision-making at this juncture, though I have found Soviet sources to yield surprisingly detailed information. So, it is possible to ascertain more about the timing, if not the full motivation of the Soviet decision to intervene militarily in Hungary – and here there is another crucial connection, between Soviet 'acceptance' of revolution in Poland and abrupt and brutal rejection of it in Hungary. At what date was the decision taken to attack Budapest? This is the most concrete of the questions to be asked, and one in which the assistance of chronology is of major importance. That mythical 'month' begins to evaporate, and a connection that seemed solid with circumstantial evidence becomes more tenuous with a little analysis, none of which is intended as moral appeasement or simple assuagement of conscience.

What emerges, in outline, is that the Soviet military build-up in Hungary – a vital precondition for the final attack – proceeded independently of the Middle Eastern crisis, and the final attack itself, though possibly eased somewhat by Suez, was in no substantial sense determined by it. Just why the Russians decided upon this intervention does in any case take the discussion deep into Communist affairs as a whole, but then inevitably farther away from Suez.

The Polish riots of June 1956 in Poznan signalled the shape of things to come in Eastern Europe. The Soviet Union responded to the threat without further delay; on 21 July 1956 Marshal Bulganin as Soviet President warned the visibly restive countries of the Communist *bloc* that though '. . . every country should go its own way to socialism . . . we cannot permit this to be used to break up the solidarity of the camp of peace'. That stretched a firm and forbidding line across any political or national ambitions that might be brewing up. The Poles under Gomulka, for all their turbulence, stayed within it.

The Hungarians, swept headlong by their revolution, did not. Moscow accepted the Polish Revolution since it remained, for all its 'national Communism', fixed under Communist control; precisely because the Hungarian Revolution did not remain under this control, because it became avowedly non-Communist and sought explicitly to withdraw from the Soviet *bloc*, Moscow was impelled to destroy it, if only for the reason that the dangers of leaving it intact were manifestly too great. Those are the accepted generalities of the case, and the Soviet limit to any disturbance of the *status quo* was staked out long before, and independently of, any external crisis. But on what time-scale was this applied to Hungary, and to what degree did this impinge upon the Suez crisis, or conversely, Suez upon Soviet intentions?

The first really decisive point is 28 October, when Imre Nagy had attained real power and when it became apparent that there was to be no 'containment' of the revolution such as Gomulka had practised in Poland. Pro-Soviet leaders of the Hungarian Communist Party had already been removed, ironically enough by the Russians themselves.

Already on 23 October, with Budapest in a turmoil of spontaneous popular demonstrations, the Government had its back to the wall; that evening, the giant statue of Stalin was hacked down, but in the early hours of 24 October – at about 2 a.m. – the first Soviet combat troops appeared in the Hungarian capital, the tanks of the 2nd Guards Mechanized Division. This first intervention was subsequently explained away with the assertion that the Hungarian Central Committee (which had elected Imre Nagy Prime Minister) had 'requested' Soviet military assistance at the evening session of 23 October. For his part, Imre Nagy later denied that he had called in the Soviet Army, which, it is worth noting, must have done some fantastically fast driving with its tanks if the tale of the 'request' and its fulfilment is to make sense within the margin of these few hours. Four divisions were moved up, 2nd Mechanized into Budapest, 17th Mechanized into Western Hungary, and the 32nd and 34th Mechanized Divisions came in from Rumania.

The first Soviet military operations against the Budapest insurgents began on 24 October, when 2nd Mechanized tanks opened fire in Budapest: the next day Soviet artillery was in action, the day when Mikoyan (who had been in Budapest briefly on 23 October) and Suslov flew in from Moscow. They dismissed Gero, First Secretary of the Hungarian Party, who was bundled off, and Janos Kadar took his place; Imre Nagy was confirmed as Prime Minister and now permitted to announce in person a series of 'concessions' which included negotiations for the withdrawal of Soviet troops. Two days later, Imre Nagy announced the formation of a new government which included two non-Communists, Zoltan Tildy, a former President, and Bela Kovacs, former Secretary-General of the Smallholders Party.

After 28 October, Moscow was obliged to face a situation in Hungary which, far from running on the lines of Polish 'Gomulkaism' which had been found acceptable, succumbed to a radicalism which threatened the existence of Communist power – into which one major non-Communist wedge had already been driven. Soviet acquiescence in the Hungarian revolution depended on Imre Nagy holding it within the bounds of acceptability. Meanwhile Marshal Zhukov and the military command had to accept the unpalatable fact that four regular armoured divisions of the Soviet Army had been to all intents and purposes defeated. A tactical withdrawal was essential to pull exposed Soviet units, particularly those of the 2nd Mechanized Division, out of danger; shortly after noon on 28 October the Hungarian Government announced a cease-fire in Budapest and Imre Nagy that afternoon broadcast that a Soviet withdrawal would begin immediately. Soviet troops began their movements on 29 October, at dawn.

Tuesday, 30 October, was a day of perplexing contradictions: a Soviet declaration, 'On Friendship and Co-operation between the Soviet Union and other Socialist states', was conciliatory in tone and presumably intended to influence Hungary to stay within the Soviet *bloc*; Soviet troops were definitely moving out of Budapest; that afternoon, at 2.28 p.m., Imre Nagy made a broadcast of his own, following the Soviet 'declaration' which had come over Moscow Radio. Premier Nagy's broadcast gave notice of two things: of the abolition of the 'one-party system' with a return to the situation as it had existed in 1945, and of serving of notice upon the Soviet Government that Soviet troops should be withdrawn completely 'from the entire territory of the Hungarian Republic'. According to Mr Koevago, at that time Mayor of Budapest, Mikoyan actually accepted a Hungarian intention to withdraw from the Warsaw Pact. But there were hints that a decision of another kind was shaping up; the Soviet 'declaration' of the morning of 30 October, even while talking of withdrawal, insisted on treating Hungary as part of the collectivity of the Warsaw Pact. Meanwhile General Pál Máleter, himself an insurgent and now the commander of the Hungarian armed forces, reported in the Hungarian Parliament building that Soviet units, though apparently carrying out Marshal Zhukov's withdrawal orders, were 'going ..round in circles'; Soviet troops 'changed direction' and once again entered Hungarian territory. The military reoccupation – the indispensable condition for final attack – was being implemented even now and proceeded throughout 31 October. Imre Nagy was dangerously close, if not already past, the limits of permissibility: in Mr George Mikes's illuminating phrase, Hungary might become 'a second Poland', but never a 'second Finland'.

Those Soviet troop movements, I would suggest, must mean that occupation had been decided upon almost as soon as it was realized that the Soviet Army had experienced nothing short of defeat between 24 and 27 October; as such, that decision was made independently of any considerations of the Middle East crisis. There is also the view that intervention on a grand and brutal scale was decided in principle on 30 October, again only a few hours after the Israeli's advance into Sinai. The really delicate point to decide is at what point Moscow decided to destroy Imre Nagy and his Government. Here, by coincidence of days alone, the Hungarian tragedy is caught up with the Middle East, but what were the determinants of Soviet action?

On the morning of 31 October, the Anglo-French ultimatum had expired at 4 a.m.; at 11 a.m. the Soviet News Agency, TASS, formally issued the Soviet declaration on possible military evacuation from Hungary. The obvious extension of hostilities in the Middle East has not been used by the Soviet Government to change its public line. What did change the situation, however, were the talks which Mikoyan and Suslov – agents of the Soviet Central Committee – had on 31 October in Budapest with Imre Nagy and Zoltan Tildy. General Pál Máleter very shortly revealed what had transpired; Mikoyan had apparently come to shore up the new Government and to stabilize the situation, offering one concession – that all Soviet troops *other than* those stationed in Hungary under the Warsaw Pact would be withdrawn. The Warsaw Pact powers would negotiate over the 'so-called Warsaw troops'. Zoltan Tildy rejected this out of hand; he informed Mikoyan in his own words 'We (the Hungarians) shall repudiate the Warsaw Treaty *in any event*' and demanded that negotiations to this end begin '*as soon as possible*'.

This is the most likely point when a second Soviet intervention became inescapable, even if it was reluctantly conceived. The precautionary policy, nudging the revolution into calmer waters by stiffening Soviet troops in Hungary while promising 'withdrawal', had obviously failed. It was not Imre Nagy's declaration of neutrality which triggered off a decision to intervene; when on Thursday, 1 November, Imre Nagy gave 'immediate notice' of the termination of the Warsaw Treaty and declared Hungarian neutrality, he protested most strongly about 'fresh Soviet military formations' which had already entered Hungary. In fact, Soviet tanks had reached Szolnok, now a Soviet battle headquarters; at Szolnok on 1 November,

Janos Kadar, presumably on instructions from Mikoyan and Suslov, set up a new 'Hungarian Revolutionary Worker-Peasant Government'.

The Soviet decision to intervene, however much Khrushchev may have insisted that it was an 'agonizing' one, was certainly simplified very appreciably when powerful Soviet forces were already inside the Hungarian frontiers, and fresh forces concentrated to enter, making a final grand total of seven combat divisions. That decision over troops went back beyond the Middle Eastern crisis; the decision for intervention (if timed at 31 October) certainly straddles Suez, but its mainspring was the crisis in Hungary, not the convenience of some external furore. Above all, that which made the attack possible in the first place was in no way connected with the crisis in the Middle East – or at least in no way which is presently discernible.

The execution of this decision, however, the timing of the onslaught against the Hungarian Revolution which in Budapest opened at dawn on Sunday morning, 4 November, 'with the roar of heavy guns', retains its own mysteries. With the world in uproar, the Russians may have wished to seize all the advantage of 'the Suez weekend'; it took time to prepare the groundwork for the new Kadar 'Government'; it took time also to complete Soviet military preparations, to set up more operational bases, to ring Budapest with armour, to 'withdraw' artillery but in fact to re-deploy it. Above all, it took time to trap the Hungarian military command, beguiling them with talk on 3 November of 'withdrawal negotiations', only to seize them. At one blow this deprived Imre Nagy of his Defence Minister, General Máleter, and the Hungarian Chief of Staff, General Istvan Kovacs. Finally, with signs of a rift in the 'Western camp' brought on by Suez, Moscow could reckon that the risk of interference was negligible.

And in the 'last citadel', the United Nations, the agitations over the Middle East smothered Hungary's shouts for help. The Soviet Union, demonstrably preoccupied with its detailed preparations in Hungary, took no part in the U.N. negotiations over handling the Middle Eastern crisis – the only Soviet intervention was on 1 November, suggesting a conference of the Bandung powers. Only on the evening of 5 November, when the furious Soviet assaults in Hungary had begun to attain their first objectives, did the Soviet Government swing round to face the other crisis. All that Sobolev, Soviet delegate to the United Nations, had uttered over Hungary amounted to a total of fifty-one words (in its English translation), and those were on 3 November, to the tune that 'negotiations were proceeding' (in fact, when the negotiators from the Hungarian side were arrested). The evening of 5 November was the occasion for the Soviet Government to issue its military threat against Britain and France. Having successfully loosed its tanks in Hungary, it now proceeded to brandish its rockets, but at a time – and indeed this is the substance of the question – when both situations were separate. Apart from what was for the Russians a fortunate coincidence, which they presumably did not ignore, the two crises were, in origin and in much of their evolution, separate, neither determined in its fundamentals by the other.

PETER CALVOCORESSI: *The Hungarian Revolution of October 1956 coincided in time with the Suez war. This revolution, as Dr Erickson has explained, went so far in its anti-Communist and anti-Russian aims that the Russians felt obliged to step in and quell it by force of arms. So, for a few days, they were too preoccupied in Central Europe to be able to do, or even to say, anything about the Middle East. Equally other powers were so preoccupied with the Middle East that they were unable to give much thought to Hungary. Dr Erickson has shown convincingly that the direct effect of the one crisis on the other was negligible.*

But the fact remains that they both happened at the same time and I feel sure that, even though the Western Powers could not do anything about Hungary anyway, they experienced and have continued to experience a feeling of guilt for staying away from a major human convulsion in which a great number of people were killed because they stood up and fought for those very principles of freedom and justice which the West always insists about so much. In this respect Suez and Hungary are connected because the West cannot altogether get away from the feeling that Suez provided it with an unworthy alibi over Hungary.

7. Progress at the United Nations

by H. G. NICHOLAS
introduced by PETER CALVOCORESSI

First broadcast 28 July 1966

PETER CALVOCORESSI: *When it was decided that the Suez war must stop, the mechanisms used to put this decision into effect were the mechanisms of the United Nations. And the men chiefly concerned were men like Dag Hammarskjold himself, and Lester Pearson of Canada, who worked with the conviction that a U.N. operation was the proper way to put the war-making into reverse. At Suez the U.N. proved itself an international convenience of the first order, and so Suez became a landmark not only in the history of Britain and France, Israel and Egypt, but also of the U.N. and of U.N. peace-keepers. This is the theme of this evening's talk which will be given by the man who seems to me to be the most judicious student of U.N. affairs in this country, Mr Herbert Nicholas of New College, Oxford.*

H. G. NICHOLAS: The ten years since Suez have seen the United Nations involved in crises more intractable and more persistent than the events of October/November 1956. The long turmoil of the Congo imposed heavier strains on the institution and called forth enormously greater efforts both of organization and of constitutional adaptability. Compared with the twenty thousand employed in the Organisation des Nations Unies au Congo Belge, the U.N. Emergency Force appears a modest operation. Even the peculiar shock inflicted by Suez, the spectacle of two permanent members of the Security Council taking the law into their own hands, paled into insignificance by the side of such events as the Cuba confrontation of 1962; over Suez the world was uneasy, over Cuba it held its breath.

None the less, I think it is true to say that in the short life of the United Nations Suez is a landmark. Remember at what a low ebb the events of October 1956 found the U.N. Its record over the Suez problem had so far been disappointing. After much argument between Britain and France on the one hand and the United States on the other as to whether there was any point in going to the U.N. at all, the dispute was at last brought before the Security Council in September. The Council debated for ten days and then voted. It approved six unexceptionable principles which should govern any Canal settlement and at the same time it entirely failed to agree – thanks to the Soviet veto – on what should be done to carry them out. So much for the issue in dispute between Nasser and the West. On the other front, the long festering quarrel between Nasser and Israel, the U.N. had hardly more to be laid to its credit. It had been unable to induce either side to translate the Armistice of 1948 into actual, or even formal, peace. The Egyptians still denied to Israeli shipping the use of either the Canal or the Gulf of Aqaba; meanwhile raids across the Gaza strip and the frontiers of Syria and Jordan persisted under the very nose of the U.N. Truce Supervisory Organization.

This reflected the fact that the U.N. was at this time essentially a conference organization. It could debate, exhort, recommend, promote a modest level of good works in the social and economic fields, but it was not, politically speaking, an operational agency. Its presence was moral rather than visible. Apart from a Field Service of three hundred men – little more than a staff of security guards – and a Palestine Truce Organization of the same size, the U.N. had virtually no agents to execute its will. Its Secretary-General, though entrusted by the Charter with a political potency, had in fact been kept since 1950 on a tight leash by the Security Council and the General Assembly. True, there had been the great assertion of the United Nations' authority at the time of the aggression in Korea, but the decision to entrust the execution of the United Nations' will to General MacArthur and the United States had in fact left the Organization weakened and contracted. No one seriously supposed that a second Korean crisis could be handled in the same way as the first. The moral drawn from the incident was a negative one, that the Organization could not fly in the face of a great power and it could not mount a military operation of its own.

Suez did not invalidate these conclusions. What it did was to show that despite them a way forward could still be found. It demonstrated that there was a middle role which the U.N. could play – and which nobody else could play – that offered a possibility of pulling nations back from the verge of uncontrollable conflict. This was the role of peace-keeping.

The designers of the Charter, constructing it in the midst of a world war, are hardly to blame for having conceived of the primary task of their Organization in rather crude terms. They envisaged it as using force to subject force, after conventional diplomatic processes of appeasement had failed. There would be lodged in the Security Council the power to crush, by the joint strength of the five permanent members, any determined violator of the world's peace. This would be done by the mounting employment of financial, economic and finally military sanctions against the aggressor. This of course could only be done when the Great Powers in unison agreed to do it, but since the engine that they were to wield was such a powerful, even a brutal, one it was not surprising that it was only to be used when they were unanimous.

What perhaps had not been seen was that this unanimity, in such a cause, would never be realized. Even if the five policemen weren't quarrelling amongst themselves one or other of them would always be a friend—or at least a sympathizer – with a lawbreaker, whoever he might be. The mighty engine rusted unused – indeed was never properly assembled, since the Military Staffs Committee could not agree even upon the contributions that member states should make to the policing force. And after Korea it seemed impossible that the alternative device of leasing the moral authority of the United Nations out to some super state which would battle on its behalf would ever be acceptable to the five permanent members again.

So when the Russians marched against Hungary nobody really expected that the United Nations would go into battle against them. Protest, perhaps some sort of mild boycott – no one seriously anticipated anything more than this.

Suez, paradoxically, turned out to be both a greater shock and a greater opportunity. That two 'peace-loving' permanent members of the Security Council should be taking the law into their own hands, with a full panoply of military force – this was shocking in a way that Russian behaviour, for all its greater objective brutality, was not. The Russians after all were behaving like Russians; but the English and the French did not appear to be behaving like the descendants of Lord Cecil and M. Briand. They had used their veto in the Security Council for the first time, to prevent any action being instituted against them. Ironically, however, this merely provided an opportunity for the Uniting for Peace device – which Britain supported after Korea – to be employed at their expense. Under this provision, an issue could be transferred to the General Assembly for its consideration when the Security Council was deadlocked. Moreover they had a chink in their armour which the Russians had not; their operations were directly amenable to pressure from outside. So their arguments, that they were only acting in the absence of a U.N. policeman, could be turned back against them. If the U.N. could offer even a colourable shadow of what these powers were claiming to be doing on behalf of world peace in the Middle East, their justification for independent action would be at an end.

The question was could the U.N. play such a role? Here, not for the first time perhaps, confusion of language may have served better than clarity. What the U.N. offered was a 'police force'. What the world actually got out of Suez was a rather different thing, a peace-keeping force. It was Mr Lester Pearson, speaking for Canada, who reminded the General Assembly that a mere cease-fire would solve nothing. There must be a U.N.

force to prevent a return to the *status quo*. To the tired and frustrated delegates his proposal seemed to offer an agency or an instrument for keeping law and order in the intractable Middle East. What it actually did was something significantly different: it provided a buffer which, without disarming the combatants, kept them away from each other's throats. Initially along the banks of the Canal and subsequently in the Gaza strip and along the boundaries of Sinai the United Nations force established a physical presence which would have to be violated the hard way if any of the combatants were to resume battle. As the armies withdrew, the U.N. force moved in, policing the space between both sides, denying the use of it to the guerrilla forces of either. In an almost literal sense UNEF was creating a desert and calling it peace.

In so doing the U.N. was in fact devising a novel role for itself. Without pretending to either the punitive or the enforcing function of an army, it was yet going beyond the exhortations, the protests, the resolutions of the conference table. It was inserting itself non-violently but yet physically, visibly, tangibly into a situation which mere diplomacy could not resolve and which could not be brought under any generally acceptable system of law enforcement. Of course in thus inserting its presence it was bound to give offence to someone. True, immense care was taken to make UNEF impartial as between the combatants: it was not to use force except in self-defence, it was not to interfere in internal affairs, etc. But its mere presence – considerably in Suez, markedly later on in the Congo – produced certain consequences, willy-nilly. It froze a *status quo* – whatever the *status quo* was at the moment of its arrival. Thus it worked against any change, save one acceptable to both sides. And since it could not be used *against* a state, indeed could only enter a state's territory with that state's consent, it might find itself exposed to bargaining pressure at the hands of its 'host'. Again, since it consisted exclusively of national contingents, lent by member governments, it might be exposed to political pressures from member states who objected to other troops being used in this or that capacity. All these problems arose and many of them were foreseen by those who voted in the General Assembly on the night of 2 November. Why, despite these patent objections and difficulties, did UNEF nevertheless succeed?

The first answer is, of course, because everyone was scared of the consequences of failure. Nothing emboldens a man so much as the fear of death. It was nothing less than the imminent prospect of a spreading world conflict that forced the U.N. members into making a success of an operation which, in their cool moments, they would regard as bristling with impossible difficulties. But there were also two features of the U.N. as a world organization which enabled it to rise to its crisis role.

The first was the existence of a group of 'middle powers' – middle in two senses, in that they were halfway up the scale of military and economic might, and halfway between the two poles of the Cold War. The classic exemplification of this was Sweden, but Canada, Brazil, India and the other Scandinavian powers were acceptable 'middlemen' in this sense as well. They were all states conscious of a responsibility towards the world community, rich enough and advanced enough, technologically and administratively, to provide the relatively sophisticated forces required, and yet at the same time not likely to arouse the suspicions of the suspicious. They emerged at Suez as 'the U.N. fire brigade' and they, and their successors, have played invaluable roles ever since. There are never enough of such states; as someone has observed 'What the U.N. needs is more black Scandinavians.' But fortunately for the world, a quorum can generally be found, as it was at Suez.

The second element was the role of the Secretary-General. The General Assembly grasped eagerly at the straw of the Canadian plan, conscious that time was working against it, that while it deliberated, fighting was going on which threatened to escalate into world war, and also conscious that, when it turned from 'deploring' and 'demanding a cease-fire', it was likely to find itself divided several ways as to what positive plans it favoured – if any. So the Canadian resolution, wisely, stressed the urgency of a force but spelt out absolutely no details; instead it simply called upon the Secretary-General to submit a plan. It was left to him to lay down the principles on which the force should function, as well as to assemble it and direct its practical operations. The result was a set of general principles which pleased nobody one hundred per cent but which everyone could, without too much reluctance, accept. And if this was true of the initial establishment of the force it was even truer of its subsequent disposition. An Assembly of sixty odd states knew it could not direct a quasi-military operation; the only man who could do that for them was the Secretary-General. It knew that if it tried to be more precise or explicit about what it wanted done it would burst the thin bonds of agreement and be back at collective impotence. So developed the philosophy of 'Leave It To Dag'.

This contained perils as well as advantages. It encouraged the illusion, always attractive to lazy minds, that there is a self-motivating entity called the U.N. which sovereign states can use as a substitute for a policy. To pretend that the U.N. could ever be an automatic pilot relieving foreign secretaries of the responsibilities of statesmanship is to misunderstand completely the nature of the organization.

Another peril of the 'Leave It To Dag' policy was that it encouraged states to get themselves into a scrape and then turn to the Secretary-General to get them out of it – as when the American Marines made a panoplied landing in a peaceful Lebanon eighteen months later and had to be extricated, to quote the General Assembly resolution, by the Secretary-General making 'such practicable arrangements' as would get them out without too much loss of face. Similarly this mentality encouraged half-hearted states, like Britain over the Congo, to will the end but boggle at the means, to launch an operation and blame anything that went wrong with it on the Secretary-General and his subordinates in the Secretariat.

These were bad habits stimulated by the new operational role of the U.N. as a 'peace-maker' ('preventive diplomacy' was Hammarskjold's phrase for it). One consequence of them was to force on Hammarskjold a load of initiative and responsibility which came near to crushing him beneath its weight. But though the new weapon forged by Suez was capable of being thus abused its discovery opened a new age for the U.N. A new power had been placed at the institution's disposal, a new instrument for arresting the spread of war and disorder. Thus Suez provided a precedent for the Congo operation; and when that ran into the difficulties which precipitated the Article 19[1] crisis, the result was not, as many predicted, to write *finis* to this line of development. Even while the General Assembly was stalled by the Article 19 crisis the Security Council was authorizing a U.N. peace-keeping force for Cyprus, financed, it is true, by voluntary payments, but fully operational and surprisingly successful. No one who cares a rap about world peace can possibly be content with a U.N. forced to rely on improvisation, on charitable doles, on inadequately trained contingents of national armies and air forces. But for the fact that U.N. peace forces are practicable at all, that the will to contain violence can be given tangible international expression – for that we have to thank Suez, and Mr Lester Pearson and the late Dag Hammarskjold.

[1] *A member of the United Nations which is in arrears in the payment of its financial contributions to the organization shall have no vote in the General Assembly if the amount of its arrears equals or exceeds the amount of the contributions due from it for the preceding two full years. The General Assembly may, nevertheless, permit such a member to vote if it is satisfied that the failure to pay is due to conditions beyond the control of the member.*

8. The End of an Era

A discussion between
HANS-EBERHARD DINGELS, RT HON ANTHONY
NUTTING and W. R. POLK under the chairman-
ship of PETER CALVOCORESSI

First broadcast 2 August 1966[1]

PETER CALVOCORESSI: This is the last of our eight programmes. I began with four 'documentaries' whose purpose
was historical, analytical, critical. We then heard three talks
by specialists in specific topics. Finally, today, we want to take
the broadest retrospective view, and in order to do this we
plan a discussion for which three Middle East specialists from
three different countries have joined me in this studio.

I am very well aware that even in a series as long as this
one a number of things get left out. I hope that some of these
things will come into our discussion today which will concentrate on the consequences of the Suez war rather than its
origins or causes which we have dealt with as frankly as possible in the earlier programmes.

My three colleagues today come from Britain, Germany and
the United States. First, Anthony Nutting, who was Minister
of State for Foreign Affairs in the Churchill and Eden adminis-
trations until the ultimatum that began the Suez war. Next,
Hans-Eberhard Dingels, Director of the International Affairs
Department of the German Social Democratic Party. Finally,
William Polk, Professor of History and Director of the Middle
Eastern Studies Center in the University of Chicago, and
formerly a member of the Policy Planning Council in the
State Department.

I think, gentlemen, that we should address ourselves principally to the consequences of Suez in the international field but

---

[1] Under the title *International Judgement*.

I would like to devote just a few minutes at the beginning to consequences in this country. What were the principal consequences?

ANTHONY NUTTING: The immediate consequences in this country, of course, were the fall of Eden himself, partly due to ill-health and partly due to the failure of his policy; and the arrival in his place at Number 10 Downing Street of Mr Harold Macmillan. Superficially, of course, it might seem that the consequences of Suez were not very drastically felt by the British public, by the British electorate, because not very long after Macmillan took over he won a sensational victory at the polls, doubling the Conservative majority of 50, to 100 seats. But I think this was more superficial than real. I think, deep down, Suez had a very big impact and a particularly big impact on young people who realized that this was something of a watershed in British history; and that it had taught us the salutory lesson that you cannot apply any longer in the twentieth century a nineteenth-century policy of Imperialism.

CALVOCORESSI: Professor Polk, you were looking at us from the outside. What do you think about the impact on this country?

W. R. POLK: I think the watershed point is an extremely important one to raise. Suez brought to a head, it seems to me, the frustration that was felt in this country at the collapse of world power, and not only here but also in France. France saw it, of course, through the eyes of Indo-China and Algeria. But the English response, I suggest, was very much more complex. It may be taken back to India in 1947 and the feeling of many in this country that there was a sell-out of the Empire; and that Suez and all that it stood for in world communications, in the role of Empire, was a sort of last step in this. And finally – and perhaps most complicated of all – the problem of dealing with the wily Oriental gentleman, with the half-civilized Levantine, who was so much personified by Nasser in the political cartoons in this country, and the feeling that this type of fellow in international affairs must be shown what-for. The Suez crisis, I think, was almost inconceivable if one thinks of it in terms of any other country except Egypt. It really would not be quite the same sort of thing in India or Iraq or even Iran.

CALVOCORESSI: But do you think that it was not only in-conceivable in relation to other countries, but that it has now become inconceivable in relation to Egypt too? In other words, was this an educative process?

HANS-EBERHARD DINGELS: I would say that the process of evaluation of the situation shortly after Suez has been really a process which fostered and favoured a kind of education. It was really an educative process. I think that a new climate not only sprang up, but also I would say new dimensions were opened. Many people knew about the establishment of a kind of a new class of people – technicians, engineers – in the Arab world. On the other side I would also say – and here I speak of the approach by the Continental European countries, and I also speak of my own country, of Germany – that the relations between these countries and the Arab world changed. People in my country especially, felt that the classical pattern of doing politics with the Middle East failed completely. They had to rethink the whole situation, and perhaps to reflect on the new approach with these countries.

NUTTING: Yes. I think another way of putting the whole point is the way that Walter Lippman put it in a recent article which struck me as stating a very great truth. He said what nonsense it was to say that America had taken over in the twentieth century the role that Britain played in the nineteenth century. What had really happened was not that America had taken over Britain's role, because Britain was impoverished by fighting two world wars, but rather that the world in which Britain played that role, played the part that we played in the nineteenth century, no longer existed. What has come to be commonly called the *tiers monde*, the uncommitted nations, Africa and Asia, now have a position in the world. Although they are not united, not great monoliths like the Soviet Union or the United States, they have a position and a power in the world to resist the so-called great or nuclear powers – America and Russia and even China – which they never had before. And this, I think, was brought home to people at Suez. Through this one particular instance and by concentrating and focusing this situation in one particular part of the world, this was brought home to people in a way that was never done before.

CALVOCORESSI: I think that the tremendous impact of Suez on this country was due to the fact that it was not only a moment of truth, but was a double moment of truth. It was a moment of truth in the sense that you have just said, that we realized that the world was no longer what it was or at any rate no longer what we thought it was – that is to say the world beyond Europe. And Suez was also a moment of truth in that it was the first time that the change in our position in the world as a result of the second world war was really borne in upon us. And this is one of the great differences between Britain and its continental neighbours since the war. The continental Europeans were all defeated at one time or another – French in 1940, Germans in 1945, etc., etc. We won, and so we never faced our moment of truth until 1956. And these two things came together, and this made a tremendous impact on this country. The other thing I would like to say about the effect of Suez on Britain – and it is rather difficult to put this – is the point that there is still a lot of mystery about it, and this seems to me to be a bad thing. It is an uncomfortable kind of mysteriousness. I do not know if other people feel this.

DINGELS: Well, I would say I feel the same. What we can discuss here and what we discuss now are things which are on the surface, apparent things and apparent problems. But I think there are still a lot of mysteries behind, and this I think gives people a kind of uneasiness – that there is something more in the detail, something in the background which many people do not know. This creates also a kind of psychological complex about the whole thing.

CALVOCORESSI: Suez started with the Canal. It started on 26 July when Nasser made his speech at Alexandria nationalizing the Suez Canal Company. Where does the Canal stand now?

POLK: The Canal today is, of course, in better condition than it was before the Suez crisis began. I don't remember the precise figures, but I believe that in 1956 the Canal could only take ships of relatively narrow draught, approximately 44,000 tons, whereas today it can take ships fifty per cent larger than that. There was, of course, a very strong feeling held by a number of people at the time that the Egyptians could never run a Canal. It was a very complicated proceedings. As you had mentioned in one of the earlier programmes,[1] the Norwegians among the user nations pointed out that running the Canal was really not that complicated an operation. The Canal itself in therefore purely factual terms is in better shape. But perhaps more important than this is the fact that the Egyptians have learned that they can cope with the Canal. And in the process of coping with the Canal they have carried along the point that Mr Dingels raised: they have had to move toward creating a class of people in Egypt with the technological competence to run the Canal. And they have, therefore, developed an asset; and along with the asset a point of view, which I think will over the longer run be a constructive and perhaps conservative force in Egyptian politics.

[1] *Programme I.*

CALVOCORESSI: Do you think, Nutting, that this is partly because having something like a Canal to run changes your social structure, changes your educational needs?

NUTTING: Yes, and makes them determined to show the rest of the world that they are not just a lot of backward savages, that they can do these things.

DINGELS: To my mind running the Canal was a testing-ground for the kind of confrontations that have challenged the new classes of Egyptians.

POLK: It seems to me that beyond this Suez has rather startlingly altered the position of Egypt in Afro-Asian affairs, and indeed altered the Afro-Asian view of world affairs; as much for the Afro-Asians as for Britain the Suez crisis was a watershed. It is a startling fact, I think, that at that time the United Nations debates were broadcast and were apparently listened to by virtually everyone who had access to a crystal-set or a radio in Egypt, and I dare say in most of the Afro-Asian area. Suddenly the world stage widened. The world stage was no longer what happened in Moscow and Washington and London and Paris, but it was rather more diffuse, set – if you will – in New York, at the United Nations. And people from the third world were represented there. Suddenly the Afro-Asians' third world took some kind of shape and had a stage on which to play its part.

NUTTING: Yes, and I think this is one of the points on which a great deal of misunderstanding and lack of understanding, of the Arab world in particular, has arisen. Although these people are backward in terms of education as we understand it, they understand what goes on in the world very often a darned sight better than many people in the West, because they listen avidly to their radio programmes and to the television programmes. They may get only one point of view, but they get a point of view and they are able to discuss it. Thus there are people who cannot read and write in the Arab world who can discuss politics and what's going on in the world far more intelligently than people in this country or in the United States of America, who have had a college education.

CALVOCORESSI: What about specific consequences? Let us take Israel first. What were the specific consequences for Israel of going to war against Egypt?

POLK: First of all, Israel did get access to the Straits and so was able to use its port in Eilat; and therefore opened the door to trade in Africa and Asia.

NUTTING: The straights at the entrance to the Gulf of Aqaba.

POLK: Right. Secondly, the frontier security problem was obviously quieted – at least temporarily – by the war. There has been an end to the Fedayen raids on the Israeli/Egyptian frontier. The imposition of the United Nations force on that frontier has resulted in a general quiet that has been characteristic of it since that time. To my mind a third point, one very much more complicated to discuss, is the possible consequence in the Israeli evaluation of Israel's role in the Middle East. It seems to me that the fact that Israel won such a spectacular and immediate victory has tended to emphasize the efficacy of reliance on military force. While no one would deny that any small state like Israel needs to be able to rely on military force, I think it also cannot be denied that this has been a significant factor in the subsequent development of Israeli politics.

DINGELS: Perhaps one should ask also the question what the Arab side gained, especially the Egyptian side gained. To my mind Nasser gained two things. First, despite the military defeat with the Israeli Army, he gained his role as a hero of the Arab world. It confirmed him in his position in Egypt and also propelled him, I would say, in the position of a great Arab leader. I think this role, which was one of the consequences of the Suez conflict, is also instrumental in his penetrating into the whole of the Arab world, say, until

1961 or '62. The second gain, I would say, was the rallying point of the Egyptian people around him. It confirmed his role as a leader of the Egyptian revolution, and was to this effect a stabilizing factor for his régime.

CALVOCORESSI: What we are saying at the moment is that the Israelis gained certain things, notably the freedom of navigation through the Straits of Tiran and the Gulf of Aqaba, and peace on their frontiers. And we are also saying that the Egyptians, and particularly Nasser himself, gained. Now *prima facie* it is rather odd to say that the result of a war between two countries is that both sides gained. Do you see anything paradoxical in this, Nutting?

NUTTING: No, not really, because this was a war which was in fact won by neither side. The Israelis can claim to have won it in that they seized a very large number of Egyptian prisoners and Egyptian equipment, and of course they occupied the whole of the Sinai Peninsula, which is a fairly large slice of Egyptian territory. But at the same time the Egyptians can claim that the Israelis only seized that piece of territory because they were aided and abetted in their aggression by the British and French. And the Egyptians can also claim of course to have been able to mobilize world opinion on their side to such an extent that they were able to force the Israelis plus the British and the French to withdraw. Therefore, I think, looking at it for the moment as a kind of umpire, you can only say that the result of the match was a draw. Inevitably from a draw of that kind both sides are bound to make certain gains. I would agree that Nasser was established as a leader in the Arab world. The war made him first of all a martyr in the eyes of the Arab world, and then when he had secured the withdrawal of the aggressors it made him a hero. It also did something else. Until Suez, I think, from my knowledge of Nasser – and I spent a long time with him in 1954 negotiating the Suez base deal under which we withdrew our troops and ran the base as a joint enterprise with civilian British contractors – he was very much more a soldier than a politician. He was a soldier leader, a soldier Prime Minister and President. And his position depended in those days almost entirely on the Army. I think Suez established him with the Egyptian populace to an extent that nothing else had done before, and this gave him a popular position in the Arab world which you really have to go back to the days of Salah-al-din or Mohammed Ali to find any comparison with. Suez gave him the solid base of Egyptian strength from which to act in relation to the rest of the Arab world. Perhaps it gave him too big a boost. Perhaps it made him too over-confident because not very long afterwards, I think five years afterwards, he got quite a rebuff from Syria, if you remember, when the Syrians opted out of the United Arab Republic. I think perhaps it encouraged him to take too many risks with the rest of the Arab world, to think that he was such an all-powerful figure that he could treat the Syrians like he treated the Egyptians, that he could for instance go and nationalize their industries quite gaily, just as he had nationalized the Egyptian industries, without paying due regard to the essential differences of character between the people.

CALVOCORESSI: This was a point I wanted to make about the differences between gains and losses. I should have thought it is probably true to say that although both sides had certain gains that they could tot up and claim, there is this basic difference: that the Israeli gains have so far stuck. They still have the freedom of navigation; they still have tranquillity on their borders; and they still have this confidence that you, Polk, talked about, the confidence in their own strength. Now the Egyptian gains do not look like that now, do they? Nasser's position was confirmed as you have said, Nutting, and enhanced; and for some years after Suez, he goes from strength to strength, the union with Syria, the fall of his principal enemies in Baghdad, and so forth. But then it begins to go wrong, in about five years after that; so that where are the gains now?

POLK: Well I do not know that that is really a fair question, because it was not predictable in 1956 that Syria would defect from the U.A.R., or that Nasser's position would appear to grow very strong and then wane rather dramatically, or that Nasser would ultimately get bogged down in rather a tragic and futile war in Yemen, and now be faced with the growth of an Islamic alliance against him. Judged from the perspective of 1956, he snatched a very considerable victory from a perfectly obvious defeat and, as Mr Nutting suggests, he did it precisely by showing the magnitude of the enemy's raid against him and also by the maintenance of an extraordinary calm and by a really very skilful playing with the politics of warfare. I think that one tangible gain that he still has despite the ebb and flow of his popularity is that he remains today *the* Arab political figure on the world scene; and there simply is no other and has been no other since the Suez crisis. The things that made Egypt important to the Arabs at the time of the Suez crisis remain today the important factor. Egypt has a gross national product fifty per cent larger than all of the other Middle Eastern Arab States. It has a population twice as large. It is the place where educated Arabs go for their cultural and political stimulus. It is the leader of the Middle Eastern Arab countries; and it remains so despite the rebuffs that Nasser has faced, despite Yemen, despite all the other problems he has had, despite his rivalry with Iraq and so forth.

CALVOCORESSI: Who else gained? If there were gains of certain kinds in Israel, and gains of another kind in Egypt and to Nasser personally, what about the British? Was it a total failure for them, or have there been gains on the British side too?

NUTTING: I would say there were gains in knowledge more than in any other respect.

DINGELS: I agree with Mr Nutting. I would also say that for Continental European public opinion it was a reassessment of the situation. From now on it is a new level on which we have to operate in new dealings with the Arab world. This I would say was a lesson we carried home.

NUTTING: May I quote a great Imperialist poet in the English language, Rudyard Kipling, who wrote after the South African war:

> Let us admit it fairly,
> As a business people should.
> We have had no end of a lesson!
> It will do us no end of good.

CALVOCORESSI: Polk, what have you to say on this one?

POLK: Suez seems to me above all else to show that the new powers of the Middle East and specifically Nasser's Egypt could only live in the interstices of the great power struggle, and that the Cold War was the natural environment for a country such as Egypt. And, therefore, that above all else Nasser must prevent the Middle East from again becoming a Western preserve, because a Nasser in the Western preserve could not exist. And that therefore the Soviet Union was able relatively simply and relatively easily after the Suez crisis enormously to expand the process which was begun in the so-called Czech arms deal before, and was able to move into all sorts of positions not only in Egypt but in Syria and Iraq and Algeria and other somewhat comparable situations; because from the point of view of the local leaders, this was very useful. This lesson had been very forcibly driven home to them by the Suez crisis.

CALVOCORESSI: What about the Americans?

POLK: I think one of the fascinating things about the whole Suez crisis must be brought in here, that we in the United States, judging from the published documents, had an incredibly narrow view of the process of politics in the Middle

East; and Suez jolted us very sharply. If one goes back and reads the documents of that period, it is extraordinary how little they reflect an appreciation of what was actually happening *in* the Middle East, and the change in the nature of power – the kinds of things that we have been talking about here: the growth of a new class of a people, a new kind of social organization, and definitely the new politics. It was a dramatic cap to a previous period that Suez perhaps can be most fairly summarized as being, and it shook us all. It woke us up to new kinds of changes. In the United States perhaps we started off with the wrong foot after this period with the Eisenhower doctrine – which was essentially a reaffirmation of the importance to us in the perspective of the Cold War of the Middle East – rather than a new Middle East policy. I think there can be no doubt that following the Suez crisis we came to see much more clearly that we must operate more in terms of the nature of social change in the area than we had before, and so we began a very much larger aid programme.

CALVOCORESSI: It seems to me you are all saying that so far as outside powers are concerned, Suez was a useful educative process. A jolly expensive form of education?

NUTTING: Well it *was* an expensive education, because at the time I remember in Britain and France, and I think also to some extent in the United States, there was a very strong feeling, a very great fear, based on the adage that nature abhors a vacuum, that when British and American power was gradually being whittled down and eliminated in the Middle East, some great power must move in. This suggested to us at the time that the Russians would move in and, just as Lord Palmerston feared that Mohammed Ali was going to let the Russians in in the nineteenth century, so Anthony Eden feared that Nasser was going to let the Russians in in the 1950s.

CALVOCORESSI: Or alternatively that Arab anarchy would simply let the Russians in?

NUTTING: Yes, indeed. The departure of British influence, we assumed in our arrogant way, must mean anarchy in the Arab world, and the Russians moving in. Whereas everything that has happened since Suez, such as the fact that the Russians have been rebuffed in their efforts in Iraq – the downfall of the Kassem régime meant this if it meant anything – suggests that whether or not nature abhors a vacuum, the Middle East seems to abhor the great power *blocs*. For these neutral blocks of states, such as the Arab world presents today, are determined to stand on their own, and they are not going to be filled with Russian or British or French or American influence.

CALVOCORESSI: And are they right about this? No doubt that is what they want, but what is it – from the other end – that the Russians want? Do they want to move into the Middle East? After all they put a lot of weapons into Sinai at one time, did they not? And it has been suggested[1] that perhaps they had in mind as early as the mid-fifties of this century to establish in the Eastern Mediterranean something that we would now call a Cuba. Were they trying to get hold of real estate in the Middle East and establish a naval base? The Russians are successors of the British, just as the British had been the successors of the Turks.

DINGELS: I think that perhaps one has to differentiate two things, when viewing the long-range policies of the Soviet Union. Certainly in the mid-fifties there was a school of thought in the Soviet Union which thought of establishing bases as a kind of a base from which they could switch over from the Middle East perhaps to Africa. But I think at the moment the Soviet Union is much more concerned with having a kind of *status quo* in the Middle East. That means having an area where there are uncertainties, and all this

[1] *Programme III.*

kind of thing; but I doubt very much whether they are now intent or bound for moving in, in establishing a base.

NUTTING: I agree with that and for two reasons: first because they have learnt their lessons perhaps quicker than most people in the Middle East, and they were taught a very salutary one when the Kassem régime fell in Iraq; and secondly because of their troubles with China. I do not think they want trouble in the Middle East. They may want the pot to be kept simmering, but I don't think they want it to boil over.

CALVOCORESSI: This brings us to something we have not yet mentioned: the Dam, which with the Canal was one of the starting points of the whole Suez affair. The Dam has now been built, and it was built with Russian assistance. Who has gained, and who has lost? Have the Russians gained from their participation in the building of the Dam, the help they gave the Egyptians? Have the Americans proved to be wise in dropping what might have become an embarrassing financial commitment, which would have led them into trouble in Egypt rather than to good will?

NUTTING: To my mind the Dam is a sort of thing over which you cannot win. If you do not build the Dam, you get the odium of being disinterested; if you do build the Dam – well you did not really build it, because it was the Egyptians that built it. They are not going to admit that you built it; or the Russians built it, or the Americans, or the Chinese, or anybody else. It is their Dam and they built it. It was their labour. In the same way they built the Canal – how much did we hear about how much was spent and what the cost of Egyptian lives was and so on at the time of nationalization of the Canal? They built the Canal, they built the High Dam at Aswan, they built the other Dam at Aswan; and Russians have got practically no credit so far as the Egyptian public are concerned for building the Dam. But at the same time Britain and the United States got a considerable amount of odium for having run out on the negotiations for the loan which was going to help to build the Dam.

CALVOCORESSI: Do you agree with that, Polk?

POLK: Yes, I think very largely so. I would like to pick up the two sides of this – the economic, and the symbolic importance of the High Dam. On the economic side, I think it has to be admitted by everyone that the High Dam has been very disappointing. The amount of land that will be irrigated is very much less than the original estimates, and the amount of electricity generated will have to be considerably less than the original estimates also – otherwise there will be a terrible wastage of water. But the real importance of the High Dam, I suspect, is symbolic. This is the new development of Egypt. It is the symbol of the régime and on this the Egyptian Government simply had to continue; no matter where it got its aid from it had to get it. I am sure the Egyptians are very grateful indeed to the Soviet Union for what happened. Now whether this can be translated into any kind of political gain is another issue. But the last point to be mentioned, I think, about the High Dam goes back to an earlier point: that the High Dam was the school, above all other schools, in which this new kind of Egyptian was trained – the engineer, the technician, the foreman are all the graduates of the High Dam. It is in this way this project looms perhaps larger than any other in the post-Suez stockade.

DINGELS: I subscribe to what Professor Polk said. I would also say that there is one factor, even if it does not amount to very much in the Middle East area we are discussing at the moment, that is this kind of solidarity factor, which I would say accounts for the Soviet Union having given assistance, and so on.

CALVOCORESSI: Solidarity, you mean, between the Soviet Union and Egypt.

DINGELS: With Egypt, yes. And perhaps this counts far more

outside the Middle East – in other parts of the third world – perhaps in Egypt itself. This is where there is a special gain for the Soviet Union.

NUTTING: Yes, but I think where the Russians gain the most in Egypt is, for instance, when they buy the cotton crop and they bail out the Egyptian cotton farmer. I think that is the kind of rescue operation which earns Russia a great deal more than the High Dam will ever do, because just as Professor Polk has said, the High Dam is so much involved with the prestige of the régime and the prestige of Gamal Abdel Nasser himself that the régime cannot possibly admit to the Egyptian public that this was built by anybody but Egypt. It must have been an Egyptian creation, the High Dam. But where the cotton crop is concerned, they can well afford to say: Well now here are the Russians, they are our benefactors, these are the people who are helping us to buy our cotton crop. Never mind what the Russians do with it, they can put it all at the bottom of the Black Sea, but the important thing is they buy it – and they usually leave it to the very last minute when the Egyptians are literally on their knees and don't know what to do and then they come along and bail them out. This is the sort of thing that makes friends and influences people.

CALVOCORESSI: I want to move from all this to a completely different point, and that is this. When people think of the Middle East – most people in our countries at any rate – they think of it as a part of the world which is above all a forum for conflict between Arabs and Jews, and that this has become a semi-permanent feature of the landscape, that it has involved other people on more than one occasion. Everybody knows that, despite the fact that we may have a certain amount of tranquillity on frontiers which we have talked about, Arabs and Israel are not at peace and go on talking a great deal about making war – if not now, at any rate some time in the future. Now what has been the effect of the

Suez war of ten years ago on all this? What has been the impact of that war on the chances of a settlement between Arab and Israel?

NUTTING: One of the worst things that happened at Suez – one of the most damaging things that happened at Suez – was the fact that Britain and France coming in behind Israel when the Israelis attacked on 29 October confirmed to every thinking Arab his worst suspicions: that Israel had been established as a State in the Middle East, financed, peopled and organized by Western money, by Western agencies, by Western governments and as a beachhead from which the West would come back one day and reconquer and re-occupy their world. Now we may say that this is nonsense, that the State of Israel grew out of Hitler's persecution of the Jews in the war. We say this, but the Arabs cannot get out of their minds in the first place that Britain took the Palestine Mandate as a straight act of military imperialism under the cover of the Balfour Declaration at the end of the first world war. And because we took the Mandate in order to have a military base in Palestine to defend the Suez Canal, so they believed that we established the State of Israel together with France and the United States, who were our principal partners in the enterprise, as a military base once again from which we would at least maintain a sphere of influence in the Arab world, or better still come back and reconquer the Arab world. The fact that Israel is today a Western entity in this oriental Arab setting only confirms this belief in the minds of all thinking Arabs; and we, by going in behind the Israelis at the time of Suez, confirmed their worst suspicions on this score. This is a lasting hurt.

CALVOCORESSI: Would you go so far as to say, Nutting, that the chief Arab objection to the existence of the State of Israel is because they regard it as an outpost of Western imperialism, and not because it is a Jewish State?

NUTTING: Yes, I would say that the root of the Arab fear and distrust of Israel is that it is a Western State.

CALVOCORESSI: This is an extremely important point because, if you want to eliminate this fear and distrust, on your analysis you have got to remove the feeling that they have that this is a Western plot – as opposed to working on the specifically Arab/Israeli ingredients in the situation.

NUTTING: Yes, but it's not easy. You can say to the Arabs 'Look, this is nonsense, remember Hitler, remember the concentration camps, remember the persecution of the Jews in the war, what else could we do but allow them to establish themselves in Palestine and to establish an Israel State?' But the Arabs will reply 'You say it's nonsense, but what did you do at Suez? You used the Israelis as your stalking horse, you came in behind them when they attacked an Arab State, in spite of the fact that all your obligations under the charter of the United Nations, under the Tripartite Declaration of 1950, and under every other document you ever signed, were to do precisely the opposite – which was to resist the aggressor and not to attack the aggressed.'

CALVOCORESSI: So you would say that the 1956 business made the Arab/Israeli problem very definitely worse than it was before?

NUTTING: Very much worse.

CALVOCORESSI: Do you agree with that, Dingels?

DINGELS: Yes, I agree with that completely.

CALVOCORESSI: And how do you see it in the last ten years? Has it remained that way, has it got better, what are the principal pros and cons in this situation? What are your hopes for a settlement?

DINGELS: One point is that the Arabs cannot now throw the Israelis into the Mediterranean. To some extent they have to recognize the fact that Israel is there, that the Israelis will stay. This is really, I would say, the problem with which Arab public opinion, and also the Arab leaders, are confronted now. I hope that perhaps in the long run this new class of engineers, of widening horizons, of new dimensions inside the Arab world, will contribute to a realistic thinking that they have to go along with their neighbours.

CALVOCORESSI: This is the sort of European nineteenth-century liberal view; that people get better educated, and do have progress, and people become more sensible. It is the sort of view that I share. Yet history does not make one place a tremendous amount of reliance in it. It is a long-term view. Meanwhile the arms race goes on.

POLK: Let me strike a discordant note, if I may, in this. I think one can make the point that tactically Suez did contribute to a lessening of the tension, that there certainly was an end to the frontier raids and fighting. But that probably most optimistically viewed it did not lead in a direction toward any sort of solution. What I suspect that it may have done more importantly, though, is to accentuate and deepen the sense of shame and backwardness, and lack of ability, lack of power that had so severely affected the Arab countries following their initial defeat in 1948–49. I think this hurt in the Arab psychology is of such dimension that before any really serious move can be made toward peace as opposed to some sort of overt hostilities, something must be done in this direction. It seems to me this puts a different light on Mr Dingel's belief in European liberal hopes that better-educated people will be less war-like.

NUTTING: I do not think this is a question of education at all, quite honestly. There are issues which cannot be solved by education. You cannot solve the Arab refugees problem by education, which is a question of resettling one million and a quarter people who have no hopes, no homes, no future, no anything – have been thrown out of Israel, out of

Palestine by the Israelis, and their homes and their farms and their lands seized, and are now living in camps in conditions of utter helplessness and hopelessness in Jordan and Gaza and Lebanon and even in Syria. I think the only way in which this problem of the refugees, of the frontiers, of the Jordan waters – which is another issue that has to be resolved – the only way in which they can be resolved is by the process of change within Israel itself. For the Arabs to come to terms with Israel, it will have to be a different Israel. It will have to be a de-Westernized Israel, a de-Zionized Israel, an Israel of whom the majority of the population and the majority of the ruling classes are oriental Jews and no longer Western Jews, because only then will the Arabs no longer fear this State as a Western conspiracy to dominate them.

The continuing Arab-Israeli confrontation is the right point on which to end this series.

Why did we begin? Not just because it all happened ten years ago. Not just because there are still mysteries to probe. Not at all for the sake of raking over old coals for the fun of the thing. We have delved into Suez because of a conviction – the conviction that this was an episode of singular historical importance, and because I believe that broadcasting, by making us listen again to what was said and done at the time, and by getting the main actors in the drama to talk and answer questions, can make a vital contribution to what is called contemporary history, even if final historical judgements must abide the opening of archives – and the opening of some sealed lips.

Suez was indubitably important for Israel and Egypt, for Britain and France; in other words for the principal actors: I do not think I need labour this point any more. But it was also more important than that. It changed the way in which people all over the world look at things, and it did this by suddenly, and accidentally, illuminating realities – like the decline of Britain's power in the Middle East, or the ability of lesser states to stand up for themselves. It taught people things they had only half grasped, or had not realized at all. Europeans, for example, and Americans too, were forced to reassess the Middle East, to abandon old ideas about how to behave there – those ideas which are so often difficult to alter precisely because we have inherited them without conscious effort.

I do not claim that we can, at this moment, measure precisely the impact of the changes made – or revealed – by Suez, or say where these changes are going to take us. I do claim that the impact of Suez was without doubt a significant impact which we need to heed; and so I claim that it is important for us to learn as much as possible about what actually happened and why, and to defeat those who wish to keep us in the dark. This, as I see it, is a big part of the job of the contemporary historian. The conclusions which we reach may be, must be, interim conclusions. But they are not to be despised or rejected on that account so long as they help us to assess past happenings, to evaluate present problems and to save ourselves from being taken by surprise in the future.

A BIBLIOGRAPHY[1] OF THE SUEZ DISPUTE AND ITS AFTERMATH

ADAMS, M. *Suez and after: year of crisis*. Boston: Beacon P., 1958.

AVRAM, B. *Evolution of the Suez Canal status from 1869 up to 1956: a historico-juridical study*. Geneva: Droz, 1958. New York: Lounz, 1959.

BARKER, A. J. *Suez: the seven day war*. Faber, 1964.

BAXTER, R. R. *The law of international waterways: with particular regard to interoceanic canals*. Harvard U.P.; O.U.P., 1964.

BEAL, J. R. *John Foster Dulles: 1888-1959*. Harper, 1957, 2nd edn 1959.

BELL, C. *Negotiation from strength: a study in the politics of power*. Chatto & Windus, 1962.

BEN-GURION, D. *Israel: years of challenge*. Blond, 1964.

BERGER, M. *The Arab world today*. Weidenfeld & Nicolson, 1962.

BLAXLAND, G. *Objective Egypt*. Muller, 1966.

BRITISH INSTITUTE OF INTERNATIONAL AND COMPARATIVE LAW. *The Suez Canal settlement: a selection of documents relating to the settlement of the Suez Canal dispute . . . and the settlement of disputes . . . Oct. 1956-March 1959*; ed. by E. Lauterpacht. Stevens, 1960.

BRITISH SOCIETY FOR INTERNATIONAL UNDERSTANDING. *Egypt and Suez*. The Society, 1956.

BRITISH SURVEY. *Egypt and Suez*. B.S., 1956.

BROGAN, C. *Suez, who was right?* Coram Publ., 1957.

BROMBERGER, M. & S. *Les secrets del 'expédition d'Egypte*. Paris: Ed. des Quatre Fils Aymon, 1957; English trans. by J. Cameron, rev. by the authors. Sidgwick & Jackson, 1957.

BURNS, E. L. M. *Between Arab and Israeli*. Harrap, 1962.

BYFORD-JONES, W. *Oil on troubled waters*. Hale, 1957.

CAMILLE, P. *Suez ou la haute farce du vaincu triomphant* (Memoires du temps présent). Paris: Nouv. Édit. Debresse, 1958.

CAMPBELL, J. C. *Defense of the Middle East: problems of American policy* (Council on Foreign Relations publications). O.U.P., 2nd edn 1960.

CANADA, Govt. of. *The crisis in the Middle East*. Ottawa: 1957.

CAVENAGH, A. *Airborne to Suez*. Kimber, 1965.

[1] Prepared by Miss Gwynne Harris of the BBC Reference Library, December 1966.

CENTRAL OFFICE OF INFORMATION. *The Suez Canal: U.K. Prime Minister's broadcast.* C.O.I., 1956.

CENTRAL OFFICE OF INFORMATION. *The Suez Canal: cargo traffic: composition, origin and destination.* C.O.I., 1956.

CHILDERS, E. B. *The road to Suez: a study of Western–Arab relations.* MacGibbon & Kee, 1962, 2nd edn 1966.

CHRONIQUES DE POLITIQUE ÉTRANGÈRES, Vol. X, no. 1/2, Janvier–Mars, 1957. *La question de Suez.* Bruxelles: Institute Royal des Relations Internationales, 1957.

CHURCHILL, R. *The rise and fall of Sir Anthony Eden.* MacGibbon & Kee, 1959.

CLARK, D. M. J. *Suez touchdown: a soldier's tale.* P. Davies, 1964.

COMPAGNIE UNIVERSELLE DU CANAL MARITIME DE SUEZ. *Assemblée générale des actionnaires, 100ème reunion, 25 Juin, 1957.* La Compagnie [1957].

CONNELL, J. *The most important country: the true story of the Suez crisis and the events leading to it.* Cassell, 1957.

CONSERVATIVE AND UNIONIST PARTY. *Action in Egypt: was the British Government right or wrong?* C. & U. Central Office, 1956.

DAYAN, M. *Diary of the Sinai campaign.* Weidenfeld & Nicolson, 1966.

DRUMMOND, R. and COBLENTZ, G. *Duel at the brink: John Foster Dulles' command of American power.* Weidenfeld & Nicolson, 1961.

EAYRS, J. comp. *The Commonwealth and Suez: a documentary survey.* O.U.P., 1964.

EBAN, A. *Voice of Israel.* Faber, 1958.

EDEN, R. A., 1st Earl of Avon. *Memoirs – Full circle.* Cassell, 1960.

EGYPTIAN EMBASSY: London Press Section. *Some British views in 1956 on the Suez Canal situation.* The Embassy, 1956.

EISENHOWER, D. D. *The White House years.* Vol. 2. *Waging peace, 1956–1961.* Heinemann, 1966

EPSTEIN, L. D. *British politics in the Suez crisis.* Illinois U.P.; Pall Mall P., 1964.

EYTAN, W. *The first ten years: a diplomatic history of Israel.* Weidenfeld & Nicolson, 1958.

FINER, H. *Dulles over Suez.* Heinemann, 1964.

FOOT, M. and JONES, M. *Guilty men, 1957.* Gollancz, 1957.

FOREIGN OFFICE. *Exchange of correspondence between the Suez Committee and the President of the Republic of Egypt regarding the future operation of the Suez Canal, Cairo, Sept. 3–9, 1956.* H.M.S.O., 1956. Cmnd. 9856.

FOREIGN OFFICE. *The Suez Canal Conference (selected documents)* London, *August 2–24, 1956.* H.M.S.O., 1956. Cmnd. 9853

GLUBB, J. B. *Britain and the Arabs.* Hodder, 1959.

GLUBB, J. B. *A soldier with the Arabs.* Hodder, 1957.

GOOLD-ADAMS, R. *The time of power: a re-appraisal of John Foster Dulles.* Weidenfeld & Nicolson, 1962.

HASSON, J. M. *Suez, représailles et menottes.* Paris: Nouv. Édit. Debresse, 1959.

HELLER, D. & D. *John Foster Dulles, soldier for peace.* Rinehart, 1960.

HENRIQUES, R. *One hundred hours to Suez: an account of Israel's campaign in the Sinai peninsula.* Collins, 1957.

IONIDES, M. *Divide and lose: the Arab revolt of 1955–58.* Bles, 1960.

JOHNSON, P. *The Suez war;* foreward by A. Bevan. MacGibbon & Kee, 1957.

LABOUR PARTY. *The truth about Suez.* Labour Party, 1956.

LABOUR RESEARCH DEPT. *Suez, the company and the canal.* L.R.D., Sept. 1956.

LONDON GAZETTE: *Supplement, 10.9.57–Despatch by General Sir C. F. Keightley. Operations in Egypt, Nov.–Dec. 1956.* H.M.S.O., 1957.

LONGGOOD, W. F. *Suez story.* Philadelphia: Chilton, 1957.

MANCHESTER GUARDIAN. *The record on Suez: a chronology of events etc.* The Guardian, 1956.

MANSFIELD, P. *Nasser's Egypt* (African Library). Penguin Books, 1965.

MARLOWE, J. *The making of the Suez Canal.* Cresset P., 1964.

MARSHALL, S. L. A. *Sinai victory; command decisions in history's shortest war, Israel's hundred hour conquest of Egypt east of Suez.* New York: Morrow, 1958.

MARTIN, L. *Suez et la politique soviétique* (Extrait de la Revue Socialiste, no. 100. Oct. 1956). Arras: Pas-de-Calais, 1957.

MENZIES, R. G. *Speech is of time: selected speeches and writings.* Cassell, 1958.

MINISTRY OF DEFENCE. *Damage and casualties in Port Said;* report by Sir E. Herbert . . . H.M.S.O., 1956. Cmnd. 47.

MONROE, E. *Britain's moment in the Middle East 1914–1956.* Chatto & Windus, 1963. Methuen, University Paperback, 1965.

MORRIS, J. *The market of Seleukia.* Faber, 1957.

NASSER, G. A. *Speeches 1958 and 1959.* Cairo: U.A.R. Inf. Dept., 2 vols.

NUTTING, [H.] A. *I saw for myself: the aftermath of Suez.* Hollis & Carter, 1958.

O'BALLANCE, E. *The Sinai campaign, 1956.* Faber, 1959.

OBIETA, J. A. *The international status of the Suez Canal.* The Hague: Nijhoff, 1960.

ROBERTSON, T. *Crisis: the inside story of the Suez conspiracy.* Hutchinson, 1965.

ROYAL INSTITUTE OF INTERNATIONAL AFFAIRS. *Britain and the Suez Canal;* by D. C. Watt. R.I.I.A., 1956.

ROYAL INSTITUTE OF INTERNATIONAL AFFAIRS. *British interests in the Mediterranean and Middle East.* O.U.P., 1958.

ROYAL INSTITUTE OF INTERNATIONAL AFFAIRS. *Documents on international affairs 1955-57;* ed. by N. Frankland. O.U.P., 3 vols. 1958-1960.

ROYAL INSTITUTE OF INTERNATIONAL AFFAIRS. *Documents on the Suez crisis 26 July to 6 Nov. 1956.* R.I.I.A., 1957.

ROYAL INSTITUTE OF INTERNATIONAL AFFAIRS. *Egypt in revolution: an economic analysis;* by C. Issawi. O.U.P., 1963.

ROYAL INSTITUTE OF INTERNATIONAL AFFAIRS. *Survey of international affairs 1956-58;* by G. Barraclough. O.U.P., 1962.

RUBIN, E. *The Suez Canal: the great internationale.* De Vero Books, 1956.

ST JOHN, R. *The boss: the story of Gamal Abdel Nasser.* Barker, 1961.

SCHRAMM, W. L., comp. *One day in the world's press: fourteen great newspapers on a day of crisis, Nov. 2nd, 1956;* with trans. and facs. reproductions. Stanford U.P.; O.U.P., 1959.

SOCIETY OF COMPARATIVE LEGISLATION AND INTERNATIONAL LAW. *The Suez Canal: a selection of documents relating to the international status of the Suez Canal and the position of the S.C. Company, Nov. 30, 1854-July 26, 1956.* Stevens, 1956.

SOVIET NEWS. *Suez and the Middle East: documents, a second collection covering Nov. 5th-Dec. 9th 1956.* Soviet News, 1957.

SOVIET NEWS. *Suez, the Soviet view.* Soviet News, 1956.

The Suez Canal Company and the decision taken by the Egyptian Government on 26th July 1956. Pt. 1. 26 July-15 Sept. 1956. Pt. 2. August 1956-May 1957. [Paris: The Company, 1956-7].

Suez Canal: facts and documents. Cairo: Goumhouria [1956].

The Suez Canal: notes and statistics. Cairo: Société Orientale de Publicité, 1956.

SUEZ COMMITTEE. *Report of the Committee on the mission entrusted to it by eighteen of the nations which attended the Conference . . . Sept. 9, 1956.* [Menzies C'ttee] 1956.

THOMAS, H. *The Suez Affair.* Weidenfeld and Nicolson, 1967.

TREASURY. *Correspondence exchanged between Mr Bulganin and Sir Anthony Eden during September and October 1956.* H.M.S.O., 1957. Cmnd. 182.

UNITED STATES. Dept. of State. *The Suez Canal problem, July 26– Sept. 22 1956*. U.S. Govt. Printing Office, 1957.

UTLEY, T. E. *Not guilty (the Conservative reply)*; foreword by Lord Hailsham. MacGibbon & Kee, 1957.

VERITY, F. *Guilty men of Suez*. Truth Publ. Co., 1957.

WHEELOCK, K. *Nasser's new Egypt: a critical analysis*. Atlantic Books, Stevens, 1960.

WINT, G. and CALVOCORESSI, P. *Middle East crisis*. Penguin Books, 1957.

THE LIBRARY
ST. MARY'S COLLEGE OF MARYLAND
ST. MARY'S CITY, MARYLAND 20686

086458